budgetbooks

POP HITS

ISBN 978-1-5400-4626-0

HAL•LEONARD®

Visit Hal Leonard Online at
www.halleonard.com

Contact us:
Hal Leonard
7777 West Bluemound Road
Milwaukee, WI 53213
Email: info@halleonard.com

In Europe, contact:
Hal Leonard Europe Limited
42 Wigmore Street
Marylebone, London, W1U 2RN
Email: info@halleonardeurope.com

In Australia, contact:
Hal Leonard Australia Pty. Ltd.
4 Lentara Court
Cheltenham, Victoria, 3192 Australia
Email: info@halleonard.com.au

CONTENTS

ADVENTURE OF A LIFETIME

Words and Music by GUY BERRYMAN,
JON BUCKLAND, CHRIS MARTIN,
WILL CHAMPION, MIKKEL ERIKSEN
and TOR HERMANSEN

Turn your mag-ic on, ___ U-mi ___ she'd

say, ev-'ry - thing you want's _ a dream a - way. ___ We are

leg - ends, _ ev - 'ry day, that's what she told ___ me.

Turn your ma - gic on, ___ U - mi ___ she'd

say, ev - 'ry - thing you want's _ a dream a - way. ___

___ Un-der this pres - sure, un-der _ this weight we are dia -

-monds tak-ing shape,_____ we are dia-monds tak-ing shape._____

Dm7   G   Am

Dm7   G

Woo._____   Woo._____

Am   Dm7

If we've on-ly got this life,_

this ad - ven - ture, oh, then I... ___ and if we've on-

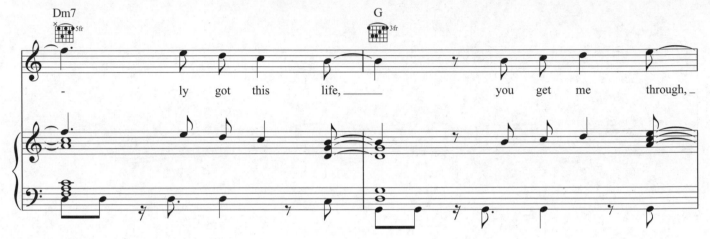

-ly got this life, ___ you get me through, _

ah. And if we've on - ly got this life, _

in this ad - ven - ture, oh, then I ___ want to share it with

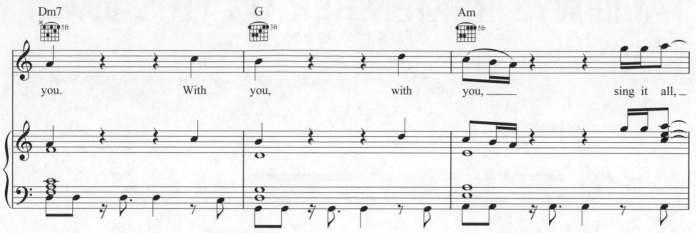

ALWAYS REMEMBER US THIS WAY

from A STAR IS BORN

Words and Music by STEFANI GERMANOTTA,
HILLARY LINDSEY, NATALIE HEMBY
and LORI McKENNA

-ways___ re - mem - ber us___ this way.___ Lov - ers in the

-ways___ re - mem - ber us___ this way, ___ oh, yeah. ___

I don't wan - na be just a mem - o - ry, ba - by, yeah. Ooh, ___ ooh, ___ ooh, ooh.

Ooh, ___ ooh, ___ ooh, ooh. Ooh, ___ ooh, ___ ooh, ooh, ooh. ___

When I'm all choked up and I can't find __ the words, __

ev - 'ry time we say good - bye, ba - by, it hurts. __

When the sun goes down __ and the

band won't play, __ I'll al - ways __ re - mem - ber us _____ this

BELIEVER

Words and Music by DAN REYNOLDS,
WAYNE SERMON, BEN McKEE,
DANIEL PLATZMAN, JUSTIN TRANTOR,
MATTIAS LARSSON and ROBIN FREDRICKSSON

Moderate Rock Shuffle

First things first: I'm-a say all the words inside my head. I'm fired up and
Second things second: don't you tell me what you think that I can be. I'm the one at the

tired of the way that things have been, oh, ooh, _____ the way that things have
sail, I'm the master of my sea, oh, ooh, _____ the master of my

been, oh, ooh. _____
sea, oh, ooh. _____ I was

*Recorded a half step higher.

bro - ken___ from a young age, tak - ing my sulk - ing___ to the mass - es, writ - ing my

po - ems___ for the few that looked at me, took to me, shook to me, feel - ing me sing - ing from

heart - ache,___ from the pain, tak - ing my mes - sage___ from the veins, speak - ing my

les - son___ from the brain, see - ing the beau - ty___ through the...

brain up ____ in the cloud, fall-ing like ash - es ____ to the ground, hop-ing my

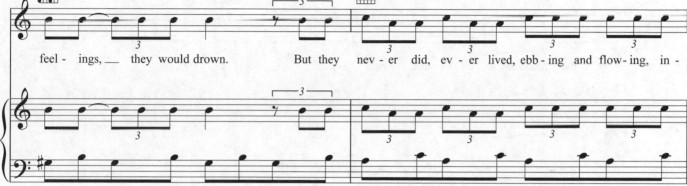

feel - ings, ___ they would drown. But they nev - er did, ev - er lived, ebb-ing and flow-ing, in -

hib-it-ed, lim-it-ed, till it broke up and it rained down, it rained __ down __ like...

liev - er. Last things last: by the grace of the fi - re and the

flames, you're the face of the fu-ture, the blood_ in my veins, oh, ooh, _____

_____ the blood_ in my veins, oh, ooh. _____ But they

nev-er did, ev-er lived, ebb-ing and flow-ing, in-hib-it-ed, lim-it-ed, till it broke up and it

rained down, it rained_ down_ like... pain! You made me a, you made me a be-

BLANK SPACE

Words and Music by TAYLOR SWIFT,
MAX MARTIN and SHELLBACK

You look like my next mis-take. Love's a game; want to play?" _____ Eh.
be that girl for a month. Wait, the worst is yet to come. _____ Oh, __ no.

New mon-ey, suit and tie; I can read __ you like a mag-a-
Scream-ing, cry-ing, per-fect storms; I can make __ all __ the ta-bles

zine. __ Ain't it fun-ny, ru-mors fly, and I know __ you heard __ a-bout
turn. __ Rose __ gar-den filled with thorns; keep you sec-ond-guess-ing like,

me. So hey, let's be friends. I'm dy-ing to see how this one ends.
"Oh my God, who is she?" I ___ get drunk on jeal-ous-y. But

C

Grab your pass - port and my hand. I can make the bad guys good for a week - end.
you'll come back_ each time you leave, 'cause dar - ling, I'm a night - mare dressed like a day - dream.

F

So it's gon - na be for - ev - er, or it's gon - na go down in flames._

Dm

You can tell me when it's o - ver, mm, if the high was worth the pain._

Gm7

Got a long list of ex - lov - ers; they'll tell you I'm in - sane._

B♭

'Cause you know I love the play - ers,

Boys on-ly want love if it's tor-ture. Don't say I did-n't,

say I did-n't warn ya. Boys on-ly want love if it's tor-ture.

D.S. al Coda

Don't say I did-n't, say I did-n't warn ya.

CODA

N.C.

- by, and I'll write your name. ___

BUDAPEST

Words and Music by GEORGE BARNETT
and JOEL POTT

My house in Bu - da - pest; my, ___ my hid - den treas - ure chest;

gold - en grand pi - an - o; ___ my beau - ti - ful cas - til - lo: you, ooh, ___

you, ooh, ___ I'd leave it all.

Give me one good rea-son why I _____ should nev-er make a change. _____

Ba-by, if you hold me then all _____ of this will go _____ a-way. _____

Give me one good rea-son why I _____ should nev-er make a { change. _____ } { change. _____ }

Ba - by, if you hold me then all ____ of this will go ____ a - way. ____

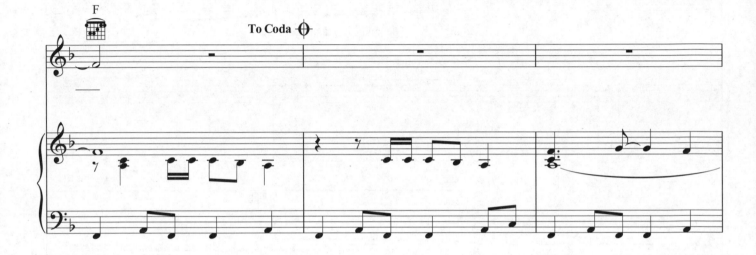

To Coda

D.S. al Coda
(take 2nd ending)

CAN'T FEEL MY FACE

Words and Music by ABEL TESFAYE,
MAX MARTIN, SAVAN KOTECHA,
ANDERS SVENSSON and ALI PAYAMI

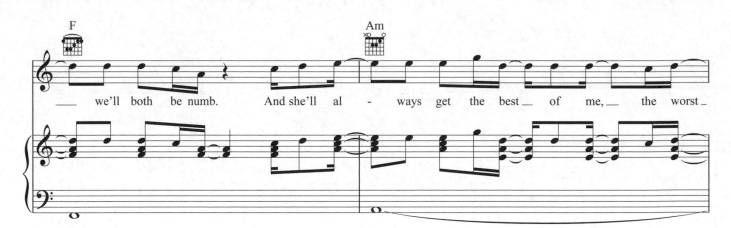

And I know ___ she'll be the death ___ of me, ___ at least ___

___ we'll both be numb. And she'll al - ways get the best ___ of me, ___ the worst ___

___ is yet to come. But at least ___ we'll both be beau - ti - ful ___ and stay ___
All the mis - er - y was nec - es - sar - y when ___

for - ev - er young. This I know, ___ yeah, this I know. ___
we're deep in love. This I know, ___ girl, this I know. ___

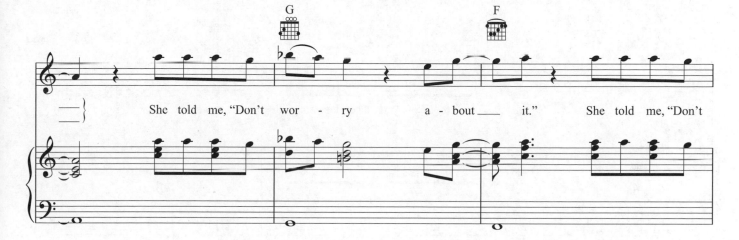

She told me, "Don't wor - ry a - bout ___ it." She told me, "Don't

wor - ry no more." ___ We both know we can't ___ go with - out ___

___ it. She told me, "You'll nev - er be a - lone." Oh, oh, ooh.

I can't feel my face when I'm with you, but I love __ it, but I love __

__ it. Oh. __ I can't feel my face when I'm with you, but I love __

__ it, but I love __ it. And I know __ __ it.

I can't feel my face when I'm with you, but I love __ it, but I love __

Oh.___ I can't feel my face when I'm with

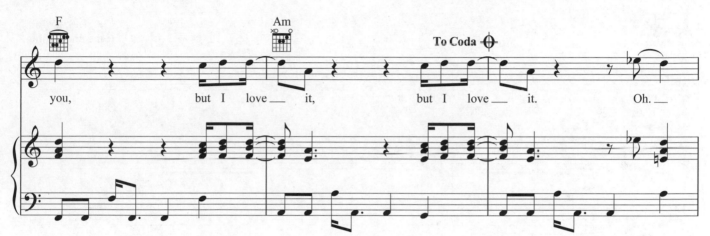

you, but I love ___ it, but I love ___ it. Oh.___

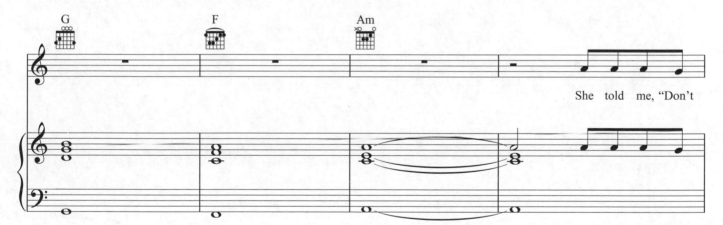

She told me, "Don't

wor-ry a-bout___ it." She told me, "Don't wor-ry no more." ___

We both know we can't go with-out it. She told me, "You'll

D.S. al Coda
(take 2nd ending)

nev-er be a-lone." Oh, oh. Ooh!

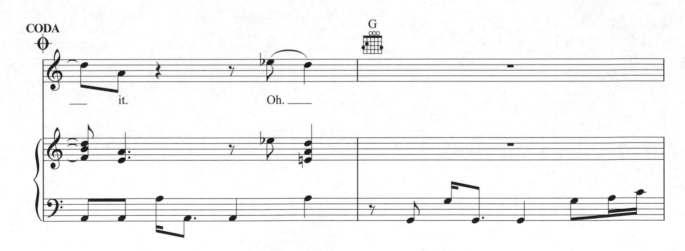

CODA

it. Oh.

Hey!

CHAINED TO THE RHYTHM

Words and Music by KATY PERRY,
MAX MARTIN, SIA FURLER,
ALI PAYAMI and SKIP MARLEY

Moderate Dance Pop

CARRY ON

Words and Music by
NORAH JONES

Relaxed feel

And af-ter all's ___ been said and done, ___ who said it best? ___
the time to speak ___ and speak to me, ___

Were you the one? ___ Let's just for-get, leave it be-
I'd nev-er keep ___ you from your fi — nal des-ti-

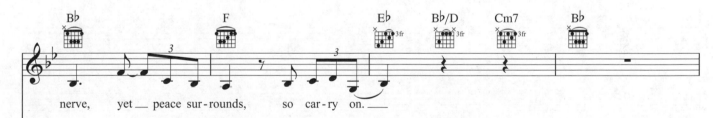

Organ solo ad lib.

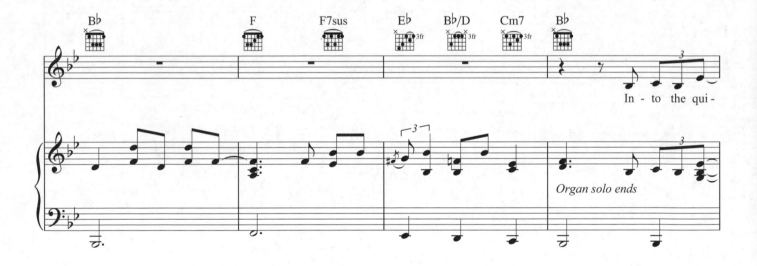

In - to the qui-

Organ solo ends

-et I am bound.___ What you have lost, ___ I've nev-er found. ___ I lost my

CASTLE ON THE HILL

Words and Music by ED SHEERAN
and BENJAMIN LEVIN

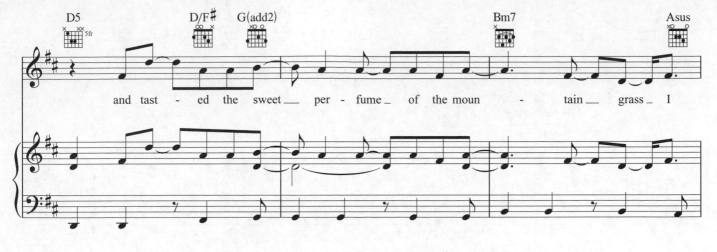

and tast - ed the sweet __ per - fume __ of the moun - tain __ grass __ I

rolled down. __ I was young - er __ then.

Take __ me back to __ when __ I found __ my heart __
week - end jobs. __

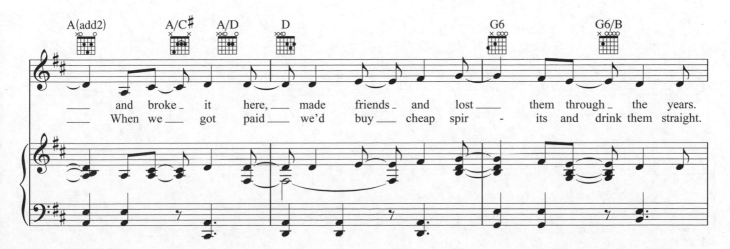

__ and broke __ it here, __ made friends __ and lost __ them through __ the years.
__ When we __ got paid __ we'd buy __ cheap spir - its and drink them straight.

And I've not seen ___ the roar - ing fields ___ in so ___ long. I ___
Me and my friends ___ have not thrown up ___ in so ___ long: oh, ___

___ know I've ___ grown, }
___ how we've ___ grown, }
but I can't wait ___ to go ___ home.

I'm on ___ my way, ___ driv - ing ___ at

nine - ty ___ down those ___ coun - try lanes, ___

sing - ing — to "Ti - ny Danc - er," and I miss — the way —

— you — make me — feel, and it's — real, when

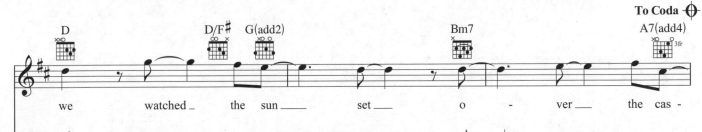

To Coda ⊕

we watched — the sun — set — o - ver — the cas -

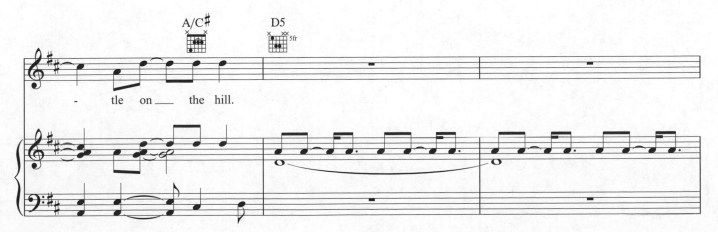

- tle on — the hill.

but I was young-er — then. Take — me back to — when —

D.S. al Coda

we — found

CODA

-tle on — the hill, hee - hoo, —

o - ver — the cas - tle on — the hill,

hee - hoo, _____ o - ver — the cas -

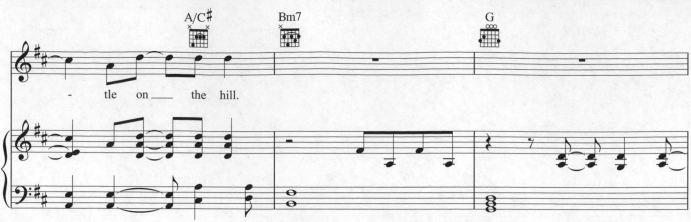

-tle on the hill.

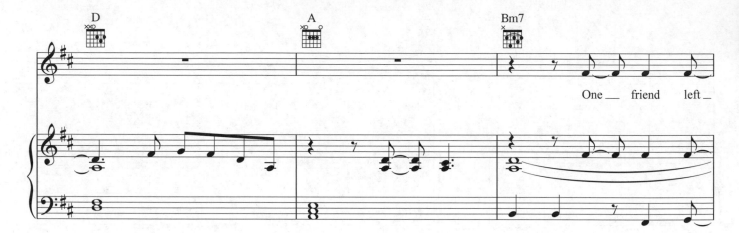

One friend left

to sew clothes, and one works down by the coast;

one had two kids but lives a-lone; one's broth-

-er o-ver-dosed; one's_ al-read-y on his sec-ond wife;

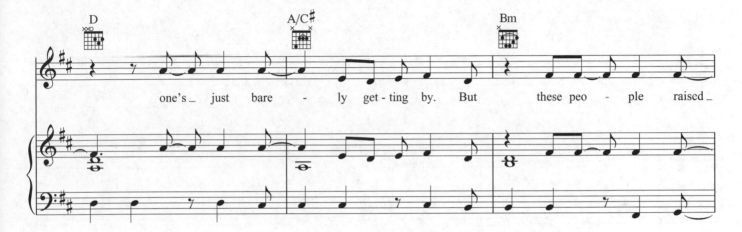

one's_ just bare - ly get-ting by. But these peo - ple raised_

___ me and I, _____ ooh,_ can't wait___ to go___ home. And

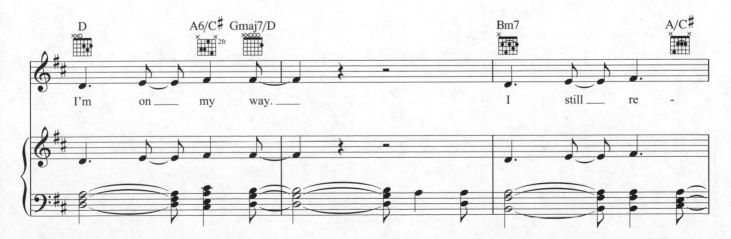

I'm on___ my way. ___ I still___ re -

-tle on ___ the hill, hee - hoo, _____ o-

-ver ___ the cas - tle on ___ the hill, hee - hoo, ___

___ o - ver ___ the cas - tle on ___ the hill.

Repeat and Fade   **Optional Ending**

CHEAP THRILLS

Words and Music by SIA FURLER,
GREG KURSTIN and SEAN PAUL HENRIQUES

I got all I need. No, I ain't got cash, I ain't got cash, but

I got you,_ ba-by._ Ba-by, I_____ don't_ need dol-lar bills_ to have

fun to-night._ (I love cheap thrills!) Ba-by, I_____ don't_ need dol-lar bills_ to have

fun to-night._ (I love cheap thrills!) I don't need no mon -

-ey _____ as long as I can feel ___ the ___

beat. _____ I don't need no mon -

-ey _____ as long as I keep danc -

-ing. _____ Come -ing. _____

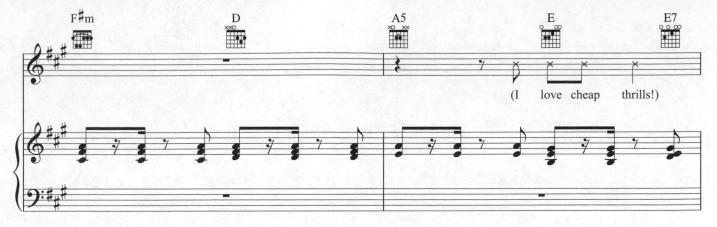

(I love cheap thrills!)

(I love cheap thrills!)

I don't need no mon - ey _____ as

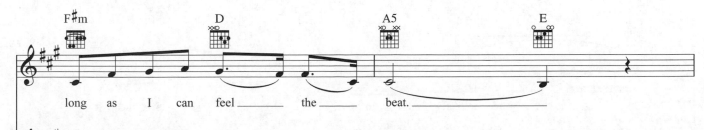

long as I can feel _____ the _____ beat. _____

I don't need no mon - ey _____ as

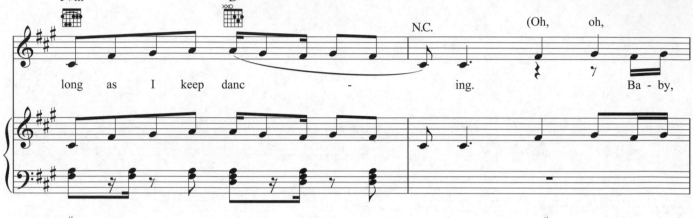

long as I keep danc - ing. (Oh, oh, Ba - by,

oh. _____ I _____ don't _ need dol - lar bills _ to have fun to - night. _ (I love cheap thrills!) Ba - by,

Oh.) _____ I _____ don't _ need dol - lar bills _ to have fun to - night. _ (I love cheap thrills!)

D.S. al Coda

CLOSER

Words and Music by ANDREW TAGGART,
FREDERIC KENNETT, ISAAC SLADE,
JOSEPH KING, ASHLEY FRANGIPANE
and SHAUN FRANK

Male: Hey, I was do-ing just fine be-fore_ I met_ you. I drink too much, and that's_ an is-sue, but I'm o-kay.

Female: You look_ as good as the day I met_ you. I for-get just why_ I left you; I was in-sane.

Hey,
Stay,

yeah, tell your friends it was nice to meet __ them, but I
and play that Blink One - Eight - y - Two __ song that we

hope I nev - er see them a - gain. __)
beat to death in Tuc - son, o - kay? __)

I know it breaks your heart; moved to the cit - y in a broke - down car and,

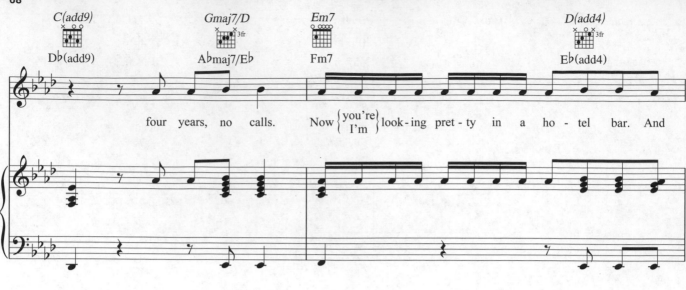

four years, no calls. Now {you're/I'm} look-ing pret-ty in a ho-tel bar. And

I _____ can't stop. _____ No, I _____ can't stop. _

_ *Both 2nd time:* So, ba-by, pull me clos-er in the back seat of your Ro-ver that I

know you can't af-ford. Bite that tat-too on your shoul-der, pull the sheets right off the cor-ner of the

mat-tress that you stole from your room-mate back in Boul-der. We ain't ev-er get-tin' old-er.

We ain't

ev - er get - tin' old - er.
ev - er get - tin' old - er.

Both: We ain't ev - er get - tin' old - er.

No, we ain't ev - er get - tin' old - er.

DESPACITO

Words and Music by LUIS FONSI,
ERIKA ENDER, JUSTIN BIEBER, JASON BOYD,
MARTY JAMES GARTON and RAMÓN AYALA

Come on o-ver in my di-rec - tion.

So thank-ful for that, it's such a bless - in', ___ yeah. Turn ev-'ry sit-u-

a-tion in-to heav - en, ___ yeah. ___ Oh, ___ oh, ___ you are ___

my sun- rise on the dark - est day.___ Got me

feel- in' some kind of way.___ Make me wan- na sa- vor ev- 'ry mo- ment slow-

- ly, slow - ly.___ You fit me, tail- or-

made love, how you put it on.___ Got the on- ly key, know how to turn it on.___

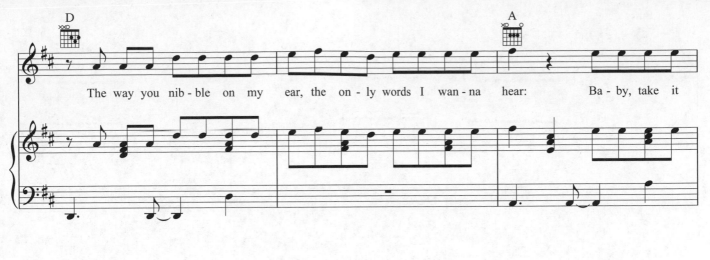

The way you nib-ble on my ear, the on-ly words I wan-na hear: Ba-by, take it

slow so we can last long.__ Tú, tú e-res el i-mán y yo soy el me-

tal. Me voy a-cer-can-do y voy ar-man-do el plan. Só-lo con pen-

sar-lo se a-ce-ler-a el pul-so. Oh, yeah.

-do, pa - ra que te a - cuer - des si no es - tás con - mi - go.

Des - pa - ci - to. Quie - ro des - nu - dar - te a be - sos des - pa - ci -

-to, fir - mo en las pa - re - des de tu la - be - rin - to, y ha - cer de tu

cuer - po to - do un ma - nu - scri - to. _____

Quie - ro ver bai - lar tu pe - lo, quie - ro ser tu rit - mo,

que le en - se - ñes a mi bo - ca, tus lu - ga - res__ fa - vo - ri -

- tos.____ Dé - ja - me so - bre - pa - sar__

____ tus zo - nas de pe - li - gro, has - ta pro - vo - car tus gri -

To Coda

- tos, y que ol - vi - des tu a - pe - lli - do.

Si te pi - do un be - so, ven dá - me - lo. __ Yo sé que es - tás pen - sán - do - lo. __ Lle - vo tiem - po in - ten -

tán - do - lo, __ ma - mi es - to es dan - do y dán - do - lo. __ Sa - bes que tu cor - a - zón con - mi - go te ha - ce

bang bang. Sa - bes que e - sa be - ba es - tá bus - can - do de mi bang bang. Ven prue - ba de mi

bo - ca pa - ra ver có - mo te sa - be. Quie-ro, quie-ro quie-ro ver cuán - to a - mor a ti te

ca - be. Yo no ten - go pri - sa, yo me quie-ro dar el via - je. Em - pe - ce - mos

len - to, des - pués sal - va - je. Pa - si - toa pa - si - to, sua - ve sua - ve -

ci - to. Nos va - mos pe - gan - do po - qui - toa po - qui - to cuan - do tú me

besas con e-sa de-stre-za. Ve-o que e-res ma-li-cia con de-li-ca-

de-za. Pa-si-to a pa-si-to, sua-ve sua-ve-ci-to. Nos va-mos pe-

gan-do po-qui-to a po-qui-to. Y es que e-sa be-lle-za en un rom-pe-ca-

be-zas, pe-ro pa' mon-tar-lo a-qui ten-go la pie-za. ¡O-ye! Des-pa-

CODA

Des - pa - ci - to. This is how we do it down in Puer - to Ri -

- co. I just wan - na hear you scream - ing, "¡Ay Ben - di - to!" I can move for -

ev - er se que - de con - ti - go. _____ Pa - si - to a pa -

si - to, sua - ve sua - ve - ci - to. Nos va - mos pe - gan - do po - qui - to a po -

qui - to.
Que le en - se - ñes a mi bo - ca, tus lu - ga - res fa - vo - ri -

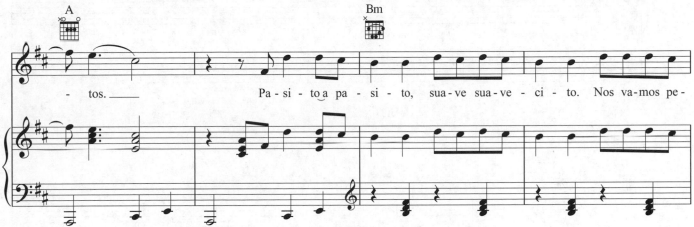

- tos. _____ Pa - si - to a pa - si - to, sua - ve sua - ve - ci - to. Nos va - mos pe -

gan - do, po - qui - to a po - qui - to. Has - ta pro - vo - car tus gri - tos.

Y que ol - vi - des _ tu a - pe - lli - do. Des - pa - ci - to.

COUNTING STARS

Words and Music by
RYAN TEDDER

we'll be count-in' stars. _____ Yeah, we'll be count-in' _____ stars. _____

Moderate Dance groove

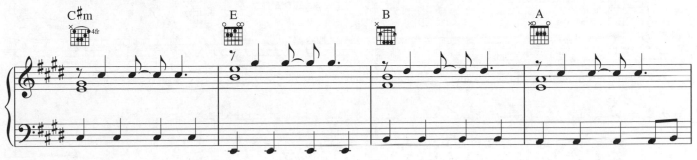

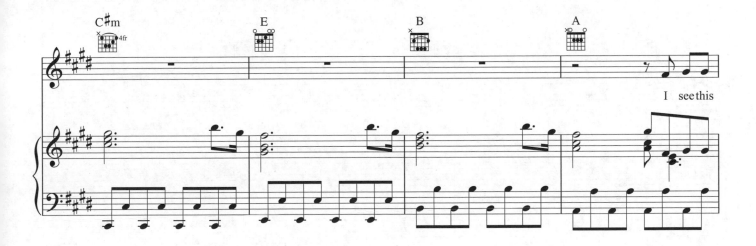

I see this

life like a swing-in' vine, _____ swing my heart a-cross the line. _ In my face is flash-in' signs, _

seek it out and ye shall find. __ Old, but I'm not that old. Young, but I'm not that bold. And

I don't think the world is sold __ on just do-in' what we're told. __ I, I __

__ feel __ some-thin' so right do-in' the wrong __ thing. __

And I, I __ feel __ some-thin' so wrong when do-in' the right __

we'll be count-in' stars. Late - ly I been, _ I been los-in' sleep _

dream-in' a - bout _ the things that we could be. But, ba - by, I been, _

I been pray-in' hard. _ Said no more count-in' dol - lars, we'll be, we'll be count-in'

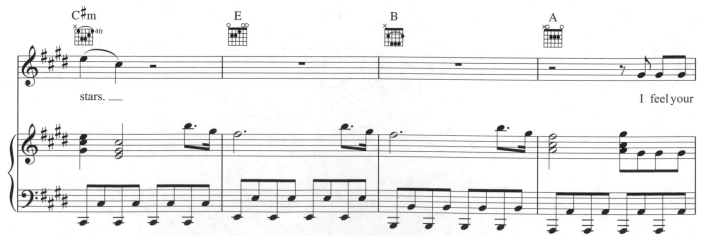

stars. _ I feel your

Take that mon-ey, watch it burn. Sink in the riv-er the les - sons I've learned.

Take that mon-ey, watch it burn. Sink in the riv-er the les - sons I've learned.

Take that mon-ey, watch it burn. Sink in the riv-er the les - sons I've learned.

Ev - 'ry - thing that kills me makes me feel a - live.

D.S. al Coda

CODA

C#m

Take that mon-ey, watch __ it burn. __ Sink __ in the riv-er the les - sons I've learned.
stars. __

E

B

Take that mon-ey, watch __ it burn. Sink __ in the riv-er the les - sons I've learned.

A

C#m

Take that mon-ey, watch __ it burn. Sink __ in the riv-er the les - sons I've learned.

E

B

Take that mon-ey, watch __ it burn. __ Sink __ in the riv-er the les - sons I've learned.

N.C.

DON'T WANNA KNOW

Words and Music by ADAM LEVINE,
BENJAMIN LEVIN, JOHN RYAN,
AMMAR MALIK, JACOB KASHER HINDLIN,
ALEX BEN-ABDALLAH, KENDRICK LAMAR,
KURTIS McKENZIE and JON MILLS

Ba - by, ev - 'ry place__ I go__ re - minds__ me of__ you.

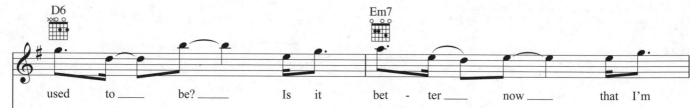

Do you think of __ me, __ of what we

used to __ be? __ Is it bet - ter __ now __ that I'm

not a - round? __ My friends all act - ing __ strange; __ they don't bring

It. E-ven in my head, you're still in my bed. May-be I'm just

D.S. al Coda

a fool. Do you

CODA

way I used to love you. Oh, I don't wan-na know.

Wast - ed;
Optional Rap: (See additional lyrics)
and the more I drink, the more I think a - bout you.

And I know I can't take it. Do you think that I should just

Additional Lyrics

Rap: No more "please stop."
No more hashtag boo'd up screenshots.
No more tryna make me jealous on your birthday.
You know just how I make you better on your birthday, oh.
Do he do you like this? Do he woo you like this?
Do he lay it down for you, touch your poona like this?
Matter fact, never mind, we gon' let the past be.
Maybe his right now, but your body's still with me, whoa.

EX'S & OH'S

Words and Music by TANNER SCHNEIDER
and DAVE BASSETT

one in Cal - i - for - nia who's been curs - ing my name __ 'cause I found me a bet - ter lov - er
I get _____ high __ and I love to get low, __ so the hearts __ keep __ break - ing and the

B7

in the U. K., __ hey, hey, __ un - til I made my get - a -
heads just __ roll. __ You know __ that's how the sto - ry __ goes. __

Em

N.C.

way. }
__ One, two, three, they gon - na

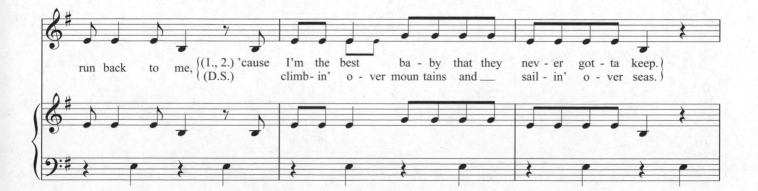

run back to me, {(1., 2.) 'cause I'm the best ba - by that they nev - er got - ta keep.}
{(D.S.) climb - in' o - ver moun tains and __ sail - in' o - ver seas.}

One, two, three, they gon-na run back to me. They al-ways wan-na come, but they

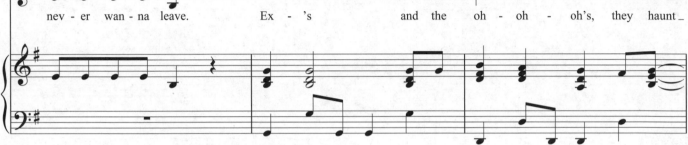

nev-er wan-na leave. Ex - 's and the oh - oh - oh's, they haunt

me like gho - o - osts. They want me to make 'em

oh, oh, oh. They won't let go, ex - 's and

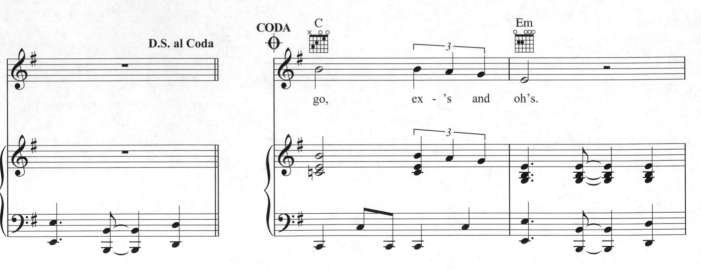

HANDCLAP

Words and Music by ERIC FREDERIC,
SAMUEL HOLLANDER, MICHAEL FITZPATRICK,
JOSEPH KARNES, JAMES KING,
JEREMY RUZUMNA, NOELLE SCAGGS
and JOHN WICKS

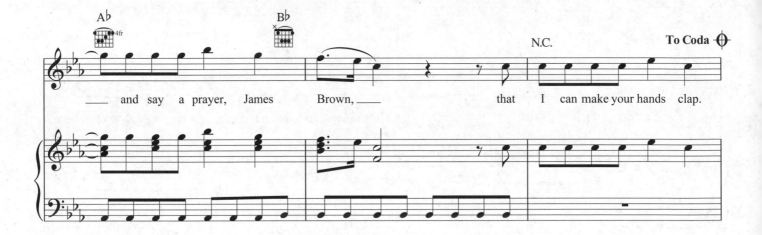

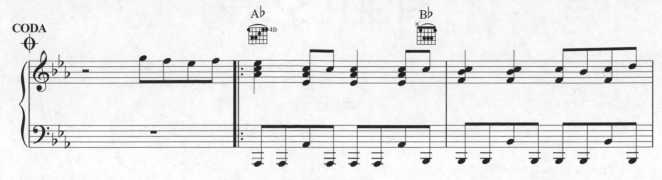

That I can make your hands clap.

So can I get a hand clap?

FIGHT SONG

Words and Music by RACHEL PLATTEN
and DAVE BASSETT

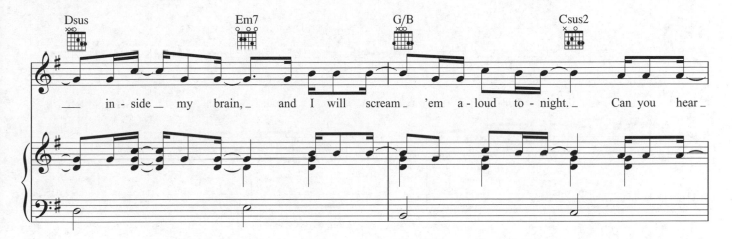

turned on. Start-ing right now __ I'll be strong. I'll play my fight song. And I

don't real-ly care if no-bod-y else be-lieves _____ 'cause I've still got a lot of fight left in

me. Los-in' friends __ and I'm __ chas-in' sleep.

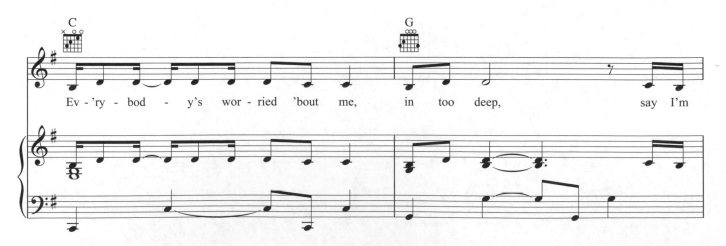

Ev-'ry-bod-y's wor-ried 'bout me, in too deep, say I'm

in too deep, (in too deep.) It's been two years. I miss my home, but there's a

fire burn-in' in my bones. I still be-lieve, yeah, I

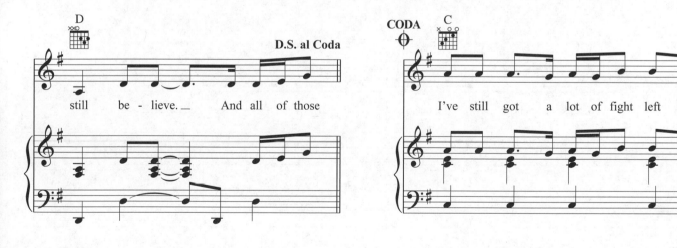

still be-lieve. And all of those

D.S. al Coda

CODA

I've still got a lot of fight left in

me, a lot of fight left in me.

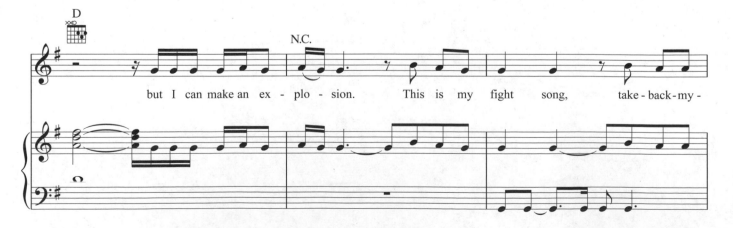

K

life song, prove-I'm-al-right song. _____ My pow-er's

turned on. Start-ing right now _ I'll be strong. I'll play my fight song. And I

don't real-ly care if no-bod-y else be-lieves _____ 'cause I've still got a lot of fight left in

me. No, I've still got a lot of fight left in me.

GET LUCKY

Words and Music by THOMAS BANGALTER,
GUY MANUEL HOMEM CHRISTO, NILE RODGERS
and PHARRELL WILLIAMS

let's _____ raise the bar _____ and our cups _____ to the stars. _

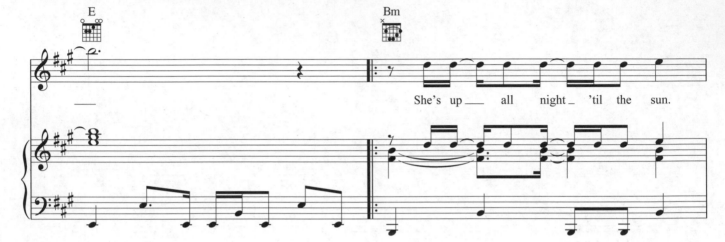

_ She's up __ all night _ 'til the sun.

I'm up __ all night _ to get some. She's up __ all night _ for good fun.

I'm up __ all night _ to get luck-y. We're up __ all night _ 'til the sun.

We're up ___ all night ___ to get luck - y.   We're up ___ all night ___ to get luck - y.

We're up ___ all night ___ to get luck - y.   We're up ___ all night ___ to get luck - y.

We're up ___ all night ___ to get luck - y.   We're up ___ all night ___ to get luck - y.

We're up ___ all night ___ to get luck - y.   We're up ___ all night ___ to get luck - y.

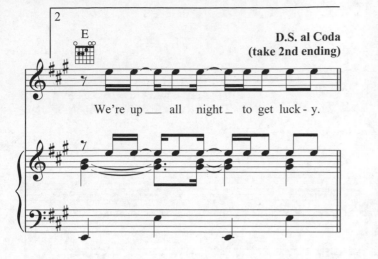

GIRLS LIKE YOU

Words and Music by ADAM LEVINE,
BRITTANY HAZZARD, JASON EVIGAN,
HENRY WALTER and GIAN STONE

girl like you. May-be it's six for-ty-five. May-be I'm bare-ly a-live.

May-be you've tak-en my shit for the last time, __ yeah. May-be I know that I'm drunk.

May-be I know you're the one. May-be I'm think-ing it's bet-ter if you drive. __

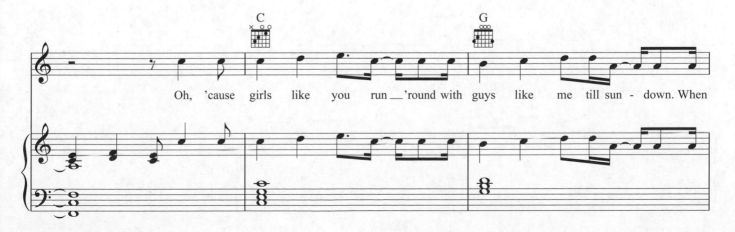

Oh, 'cause girls like you run __ 'round with guys like me till sun-down. When

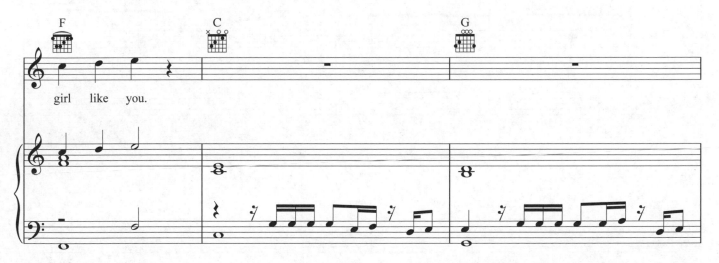

HEATHENS
from SUICIDE SQUAD

Words and Music by
TYLER JOSEPH

Moderate groove

All my friends are hea-thens; take it slow.

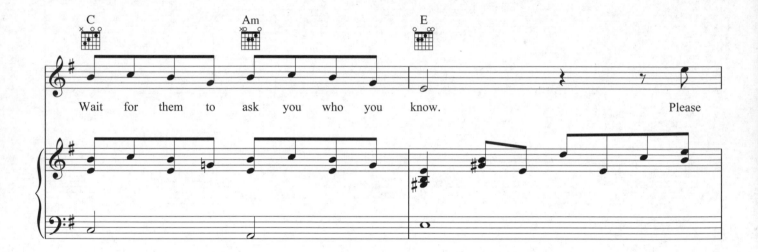

Wait for them to ask you who you know. Please

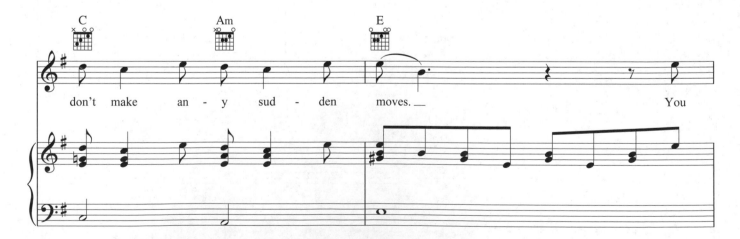

don't make an-y sud-den moves. ___ You

D.S. al Coda

you?" But af - ter all I've said, please don't for - get.

CODA

We don't deal with out - sid - ers ver - y well. They say new - com - ers have a cer - tain smell.

You have trust is - sues, not to men - tion, they say they can smell your in - ten - tions.

You'll nev - er know the freak show sit - ting next to you. You'll have some weird peo - ple sit - ting next to

you. You'll think, "How did I get here, sit-ting next to you?" But af-ter all I've said,

please don't for-get. Watch it.

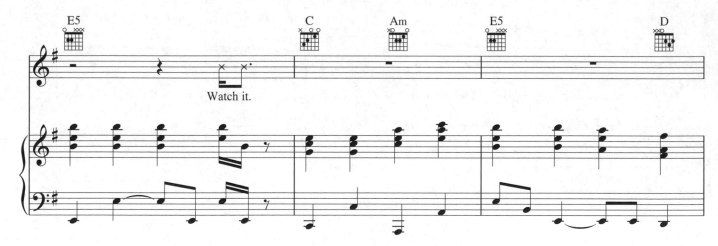

Watch it.

All my friends are hea-thens; take it slow.

know. Why'd you come? You knew you should have stayed.

I tried to warn you just to stay a-

way. And now they're out-side, read-y to

bust. It looks like you might be one of us.

HOLD BACK THE RIVER

Words and Music by JAMES BAY
and IAIN ARCHER

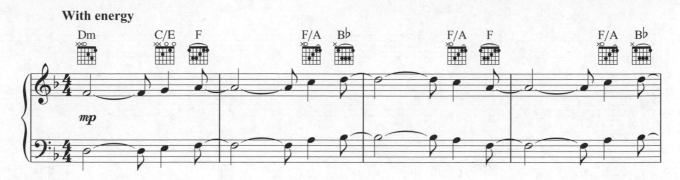

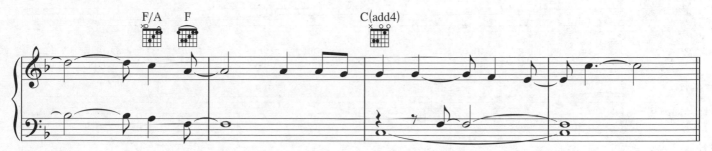

Tried to keep ___ you close ___ to me ___
Once up - on ___ a dif - 'frent life, ___

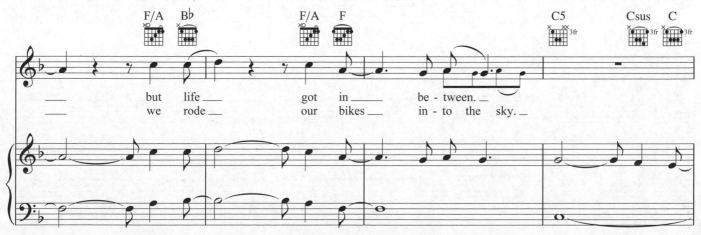

___ but life ___ got in ___ be - tween. ___
___ we rode ___ our bikes ___ in - to the sky. ___

I _____ can stop ___ for a min - ute and ___ see where you ___ hide. Hold _

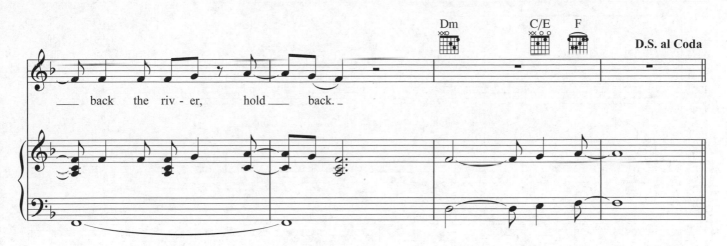

___ back the riv - er, hold ___ back. _

D.S. al Coda

CODA

Hold ___ back the riv - er, let me look in your _ eyes. Hold _

___ back the riv - er so ___ I _____ can stop ___ for a min - ute and _

-ter, lone - ly___ wa - ter, won't___ you let us___ wan -

-der, let us___ hold___ each oth - er? Lone - ly___ wa -

-ter, lone - ly___ wa - ter, won't___ you

let us___ wan - der, let us___ hold___

Lone - ly__ wa - ter, lone - ly__ wa - ter, won't__ you

let us__ wan - der, let us__ hold__ each oth - er?

let us__ hold__ each oth - er?

HUMAN

Words and Music by JAMIE HARTMAN,
RORY GRAHAM and NICK MONSON

Recorded a half step lower.

I'M NOT THE ONLY ONE

Words and Music by SAM SMITH
and JAMES NAPIER

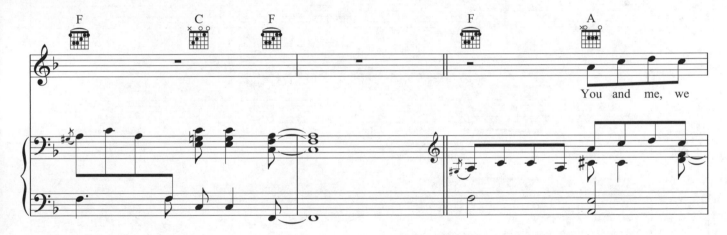

LANTERNS

Words and Music by ADAM SPARK, IAN KENNY,
GLENN SARANGAPANY, IAN BERNEY
and ADAM WESTON

Moderately, in 2

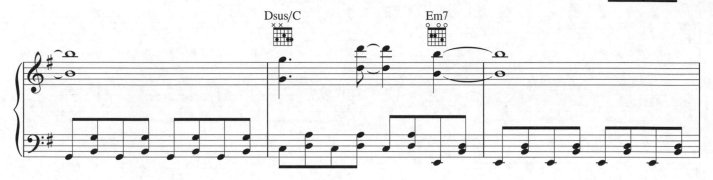

Late - ly I've found ____
As we walk out ____

____ when I start to think ____ a - loud,
____ with - out ques - tion, with - out doubt, ____

that is where I should be. \
we have noth - ing to fear. \
We nev - er car - ry days on \
our own, but now it's up to \
us to know the

weight of be-ing so much more._____ We will

find our-selves_____ on the____ road._____

On we____ march_____ with the mid-night_ sun.____

We have a light to our fac - es, and re - al - ized we were chas - ing shad - ows be - hind. Now we're sav -

LET HER GO

Words and Music by
MICHAEL DAVID ROSENBERG

Well, you on - ly need the

light when it's burn - in' low. On - ly miss the sun when it starts to snow.

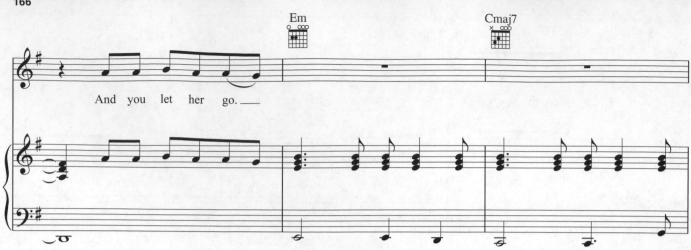

And you let her go. ___

Star - ing at the bot - tom of your glass, hop - ing one ___ day you'll make a dream

Star - ing at the ceil - ing in the dark, same old emp - ty feel - ing in your

Will you let her go? _____

D.S. al Coda

'Cause you on - ly need the

CODA

'Cause you on - ly need the light when it's burn - in' low.

LET ME LOVE YOU

Words and Music by JUSTIN BIEBER,
CARL ROSEN, WILLIAM GRIGAHCINE,
EDWIN PEREZ, TEDDY MENDEZ,
ANDREW WOTMAN, ALEXANDRA TAMPOSI,
LOUIS BELL, LUMIDEE CEDEÑO,
BRIAN LEE and STEVEN MARSDEN

Moderate Pop

I used to be-lieve ___ we were burn-ing on the edge of some-thing

___ at the wheel; we've got a mil-lion miles a-

beau-ti-ful, some-thing beau-ti-ful. Sell-ing a dream, ___

head of us, miles a-head of us. All that we need ___

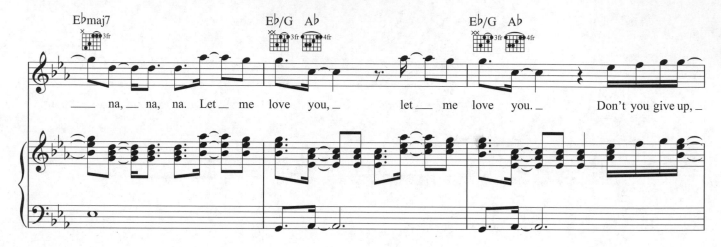

Don't fall a - sleep __

Don't you give up, ___ na, ___ na, na. I won't give up, ___ na, ___ na, na. Let ___ me

love you, _ let ___ me love you. _ Don't you give up, ___ na, ___ na, na. I won't give up, _

___ na, ___ na, na. Let ___ me love you, ___ let ___ me love you. _

LIKE I'M GONNA LOSE YOU

Words and Music by CAITLYN ELIZABETH SMITH,
JUSTIN WEAVER and MEGHAN TRAINOR

LOST BOY

Words and Music by
RUTH BERHE

closed my eyes, I saw a shad-ow fly-ing ___ high.

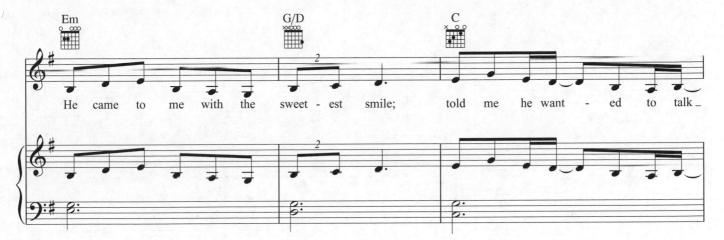

He came to me with the sweet-est smile; told me he want-ed to talk ___

___ for a-while. ___ He said, "Pe-ter Pan, that's what they call me.

I prom-ise that you'll nev-er be lone-ly." And ev-er

since that ___ day... ___ I am a lost boy

from Nev - er - land, u - sually hang - ing out ___ with ___ Pe - ter Pan. ___

___ And when we're bored, we play ___ in the woods, al - ways on the run ___ from ___

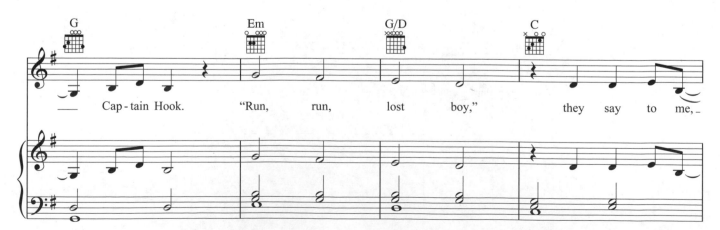

___ Cap - tain Hook. "Run, run, lost boy," they say to me, ___

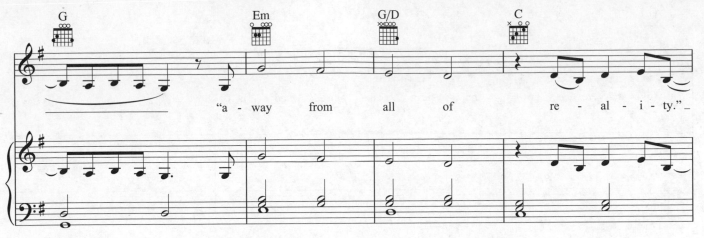

"a - way from all of re - al - i - ty."

Nev - er - land is home to the lost boys like me; and

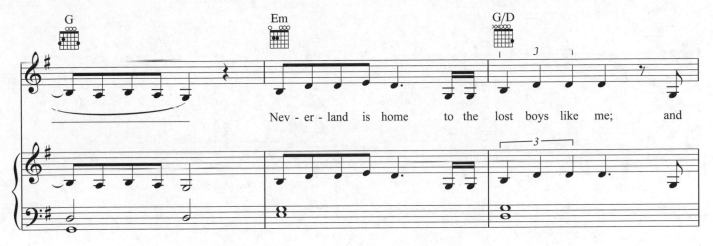

lost boys like me are ___ free. Nev - er - land is home to the lost boys like me; and

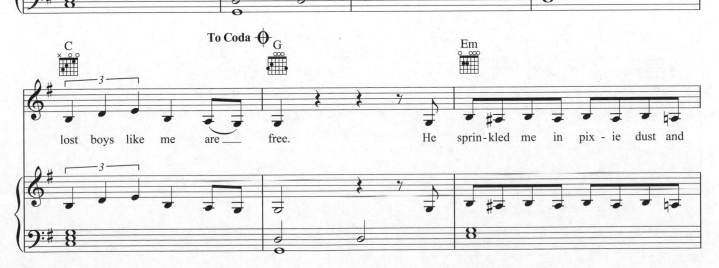

lost boys like me are ___ free. He sprin - kled me in pix - ie dust and

told me to be - lieve, be - lieve in him and be - lieve in me. "To-

geth - er, we will fly a - way in a cloud of green, to your beau - ti - ful des - ti - ny." As we

soared a - bove the town that nev - er loved me, I real - ized I fi - n'lly had a

fam - i - ly. Soon e - nough, we reached Nev - er - land. Peace - ful - ly, my feet

D.S. al Coda

hit the sand. And ev – er since that day...

CODA

free.   Pe – ter Pan, Tin – ker – bell, Wen – dy Dar – ling,

e – ven Cap – tain Hook: you are my   per – fect sto – ry – book.   Nev – er – land, I love you so;

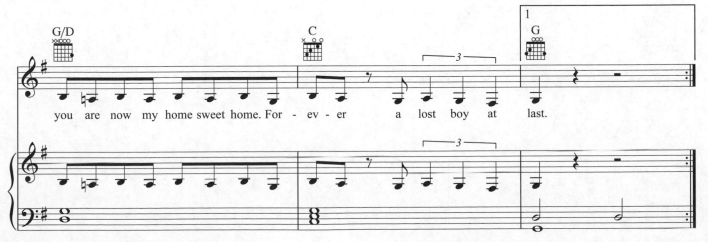

you are now my home sweet home. For – ev – er   a lost boy at last.

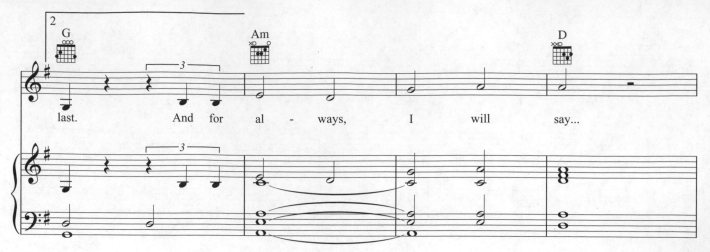

last. And for al - ways, I will say...

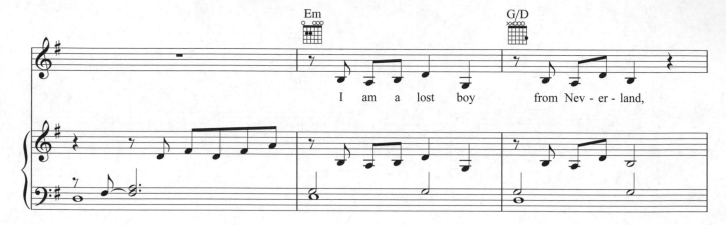

I am a lost boy from Nev - er - land,

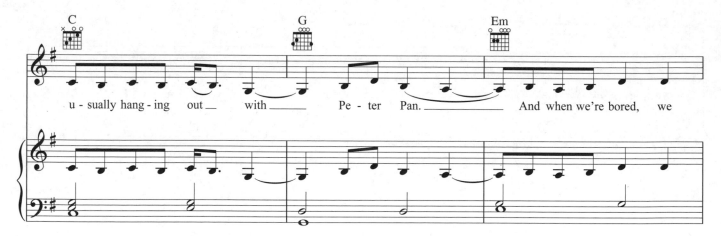

u - sually hang - ing out with Pe - ter Pan. And when we're bored, we

play in the woods, al - ways on the run from Cap - tain Hook.

"Run, run, lost boy," _____ they say to me, _____ "a-

way from all of re-al-i-ty." _____

Nev-er-land is home to the lost boys like me; and lost boys like me are free.

Nev-er-land is home to the lost boys like me; and lost boys like me are free.

LOVE ME NOW

Words and Music by JOHN STEPHENS,
JOHN HENRY RYAN and BLAKE MILLS

so
Oh, } I'm gon-na love ___ you now like it's all I ___ have. ___ I

know ___ it-'ll kill me when it's o - ver. ___ I don't wan-na think ___

Play 1st time only

N.C.

___ a - bout ___ it; I want you to love ___ me now. I don't know

who's gon - na kiss you when I'm gone, ___ so I'm gon - na love _

LOVE ON THE WEEKEND

Words and Music by
JOHN MAYER

It's a Fri - day;   we fi - n'lly made it.
You be the D. J.,   I'll be the driv - er.

I can't be - lieve I get to   see __ your   face. __   You've been work - ing
You put your feet up in the   get - a - way   car. __   I'm fly - ing fast like a,

and I've been wait - ing   to pick you up and take you   from this   place. __
a want - ed man.   I want you, ba - by, like you   can't un - der - stand. __

Love on the week - end,   love on the week - end, __   like on - ly we   can, __
Love on the week - end,   love on the week - end. __   We found a mes - sage in a

like on - ly we   can. __   Love on the week - end,   love on the week - end, __
bot - tle   we were drink - ing. __   Love on the week - end,   love on the week - end. __

I'm com - ing up   and I'm lov - ing ev - 'ry min - ute of it.
I hate your guts 'cause I'm

lov - ing ev - 'ry min - ute of it.

My clothes are dirt - y and my friends are get - ting wor - ried. Down there be - low us,

un - der the clouds, ba - by, take my hand and pull me down, down, down, down.

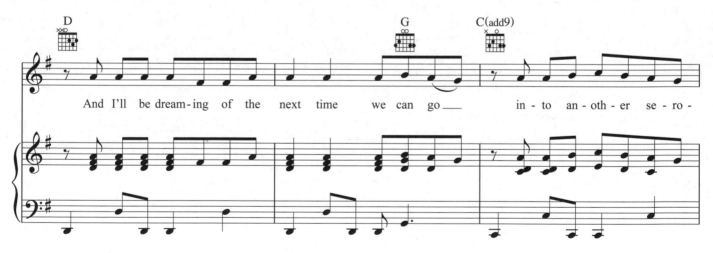

And I'll be dream - ing of the next time we can go ___ in - to an - oth - er se - ro -

ton in o - ver - flow. Love on the week - end, love on the week - end. ___

I'm bust-ed up, but I'm lov-ing ev-'ry min-ute of it.

Love on the week-end.

Love on the week-end.

Repeat and Fade

Optional Ending

LOVE ON THE BRAIN

Words and Music by ROBYN FENTY,
JOSEPH ANGEL and FREDERIK BALL

Slowly, in 2

And you got me like, oh;   what you

want from me? (What you want from me?) And I tried ___ to buy ___ your

pret - ty heart, but the price too high. _____ Ba - by, you got me like,

oh. _____ Mm. You love when I fall a - part, _____

(fall a - part) so you can put me to - geth - er and throw me a - gainst the

wall. _____ Ba - by, you got me like, ah, _____

cur - ing my name. (Curs - ing my name.) No mat - ter what I do, I'm no

good with - out you, and I can't get e - nough. ___ Must be love on __ the

brain. _____ Then you keep... Love me, just

love me, ___ yeah. Just love me. ___ All you need to do is

love me, _____ yeah. Got me like, ah - ah - ah - ow.

I'm ___ tired of be - ing played _____ like a vi - o - lin. _____ What do I

got _____ to do to get ___ in _____ your moth - er - fuck - ing ___ heart? _____

___ Ba - by, like,

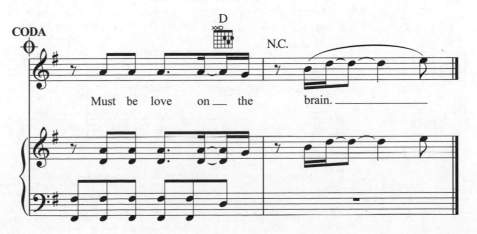

Must be love on ___ the brain. _____

LOVE YOURSELF

Words and Music by JUSTIN BIEBER,
BENJAMIN LEVIN, ED SHEERAN,
JOSHUA GUDWIN and SCOTT BRAUN

Moderate groove

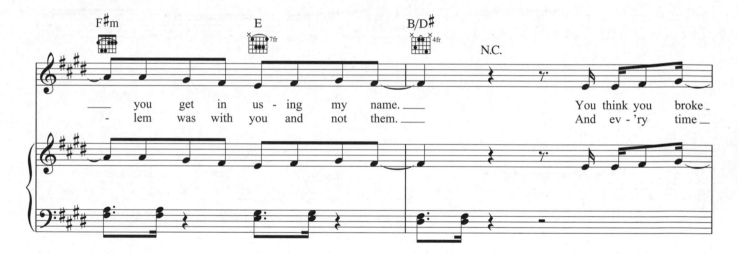

look that __ much, __ oh, ba - by, you should go and love your - self. __ And if you

think that _ I'm still hold - ing __ on __ to some - thing, you should go and love your - self. __

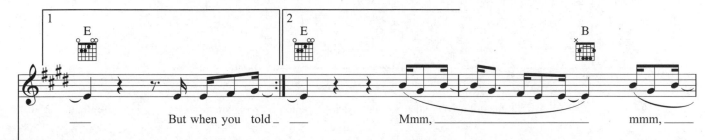

But when you told __ __ Mmm, _____ mmm, _____

mmm, _____ mmm. _____

Mmm, _____ mmm, _____

_____ mmm, _____ mmm. _____

_____ For all the times _ that _ you made _ me _ feel small, I fell in love, _

_____ now I feel noth-ing at all. ____ I nev-er felt ___ so low when I was vul-nera-

LUCKY

Words and Music by JASON MRAZ,
COLBIE CAILLAT and TIMOTHY FAGAN

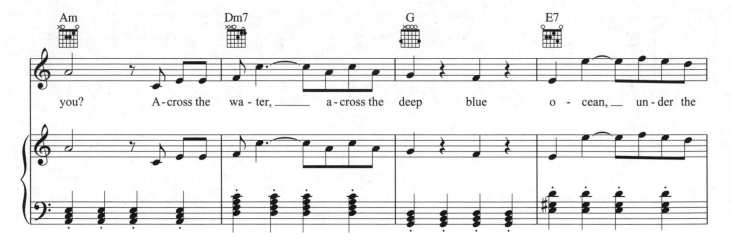

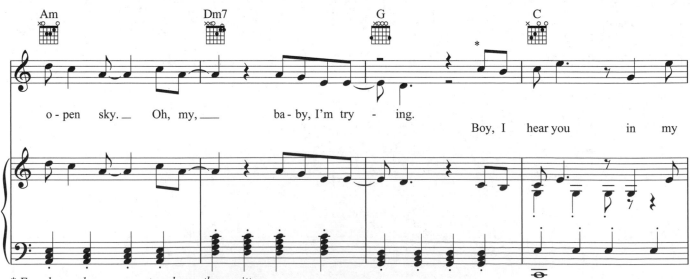

* *Female vocal sung one octave lower than written.*

*Substitute half rest on D.S.

world keeps spin-ning 'round, you hold me right here, right now.

CODA

Oo,

oo. Oo,

oo. Oo.

MERCY

Words and Music by AIMEE DUFFY
and STEPHEN BOOKER

but you do it well, I'm un-der your spell.

You've got me beg-ging you for mer-cy,
(Yeah, *yeah,* *yeah,*

why won't __ you re-lease __ me?
yeah, *yeah,* *yeah,*

you've got me beg-ging you for mer - cy,
yeah, *yeah,* *yeah,*

— me? I'm beg - ging you for mer - cy,

you got me beg - ging, you got me beg - ging, you got me beg - ging...

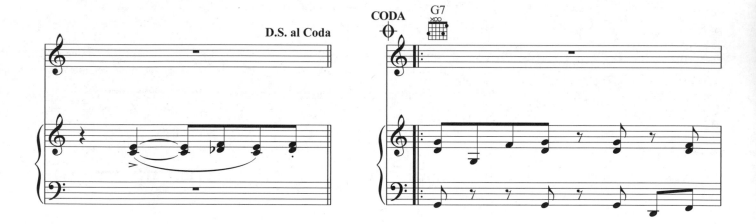

D.S. al Coda

CODA G7

Repeat ad lib. to Fade

Beg-ging you for mer - cy, you got me beg - ging, down on my knees, I said...

MILLION REASONS

Words and Music by STEFANI GERMANOTTA,
MARK RONSON and HILLARY LINDSEY

Givin' me a million reasons, about a million reasons. If I had a high-way, I would
Givin' me a million reasons, about a million reasons. And if you say somethin' that you

run for the hills. __ If you could find a dry way, I'd for-ev-er be still. __ But you're
might e-ven mean, __ it's hard to e-ven fath-om which parts I should be-lieve. __ 'Cause you're

givin' me a million reasons, give me a million reasons. Givin' me a million reasons,

about a million reasons. I bow down to pray. __

I try to make the worst seem bet-ter.__ Lord, show me the way__

__ to cut through all this worn-out leath-er. I've got a

hun-dred mil-lion rea-sons to walk a-way,_____ but,

To Coda ⊕

ba-by, I just need one good one__ to stay.__

good one _____ to stay. _____

Oh, ba - by, I'm bleed - in', bleed - in'. _____

Can't you give me what I'm need - in', need - in'?

Ev - 'ry heart - break makes it hard to keep the

faith. _____ But, ba - by, I just need one good one, good one,

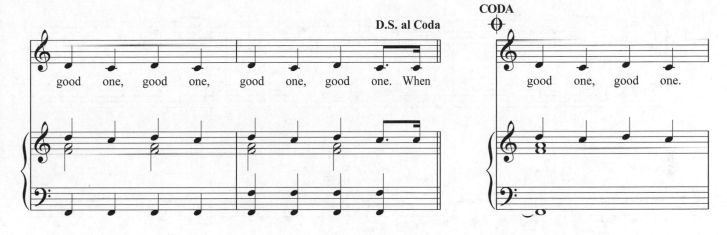

D.S. al Coda

CODA

good one, good one, good one, good one. When

good one, good one.

Tell me that you'll be the good one, good one. Ba - by, I just need one

rit.

good one __ to stay. _____

THE MIDDLE

Words and Music by SARAH AARONS,
MARCUS LOMAX, JORDAN JOHNSON,
ANTON ZASLAVSKI, KYLE TREWARTHA,
MICHAEL TREWARTHA and STEFAN JOHNSON

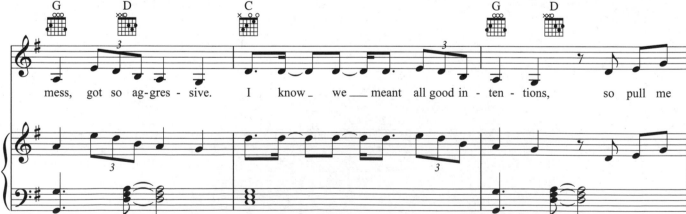

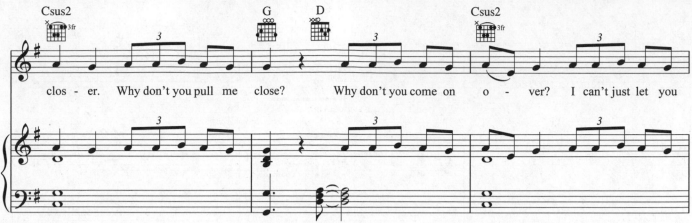

clos - er. Why don't you pull me close? Why don't you come on o - ver? I can't just let you

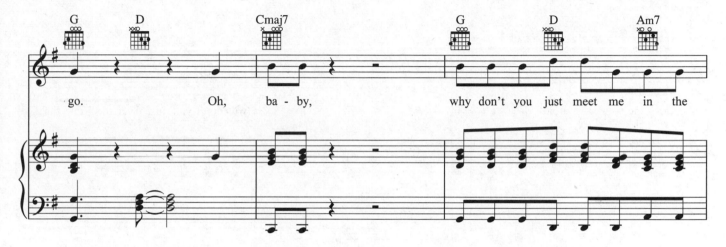

go. Oh, ba - by, why don't you just meet me in the

mid - dle? I'm los - ing my mind just a lit - tle. So,

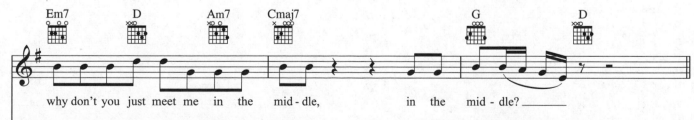

why don't you just meet me in the mid - dle, in the mid - dle? _____

mis - sion, __ re - gard-less of my ob - jec - tion. __ Oh, oh, and it's not a - bout my

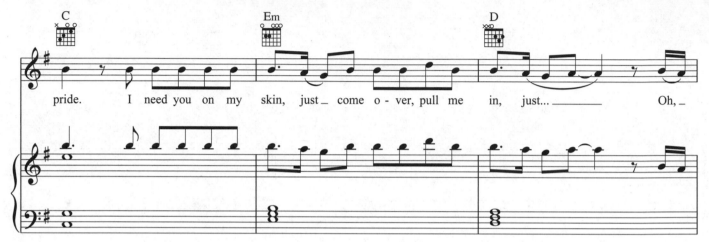

pride. I need you on my skin, just __ come o - ver, pull me in, just... _____ Oh, __

ba - by, why don't you just meet me in the mid - dle? I'm

los - ing my mind just a lit - tle. So, why don't you just meet me in the

NEVER BE THE SAME

Words and Music by CAMILA CABELLO,
ADAM FEENEY, NOONIE BAO,
LEO RAMI DAWOOD, JACOB LUDWIG OLOFSSON
and SASHA YATCHENKO

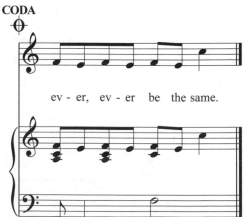

PRAYING

Words and Music by KESHA SEBERT,
BEN ABRAHAM, RYAN LEWIS
and ANDREW JOSLYN

but af - ter ev - 'ry - thing __ you've done,

I can thank you for __ how strong I have __ be - come. _____ 'Cause

you brought the flames and you put me through hell. I had to learn how to fight for my - self.

And we both know all the truth I could tell. I'll just say this is 'I wish you fare - well.' __

say _____ in life, you're gon - na get what you give. _____ But some

things on - ly God can for - give. _____ Ah, _____

I hope you're some-where pray - ing, _____ pray - ing.

I hope your soul is chang - ing, _____ chang - ing. _____

_____ I hope you find your peace _____ fall - ing on _____ your knees, _____

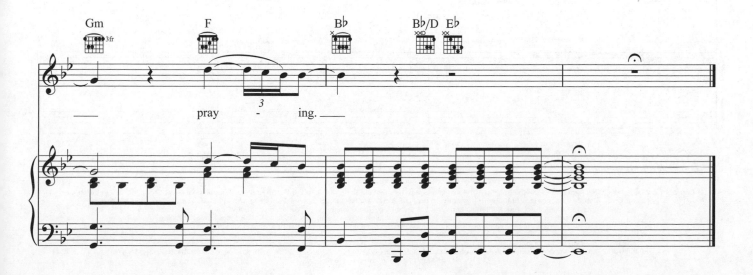

_____ pray - ing. _____

ONE CALL AWAY

Words and Music by CHARLIE PUTH,
JUSTIN FRANKS, BREYAN ISAAC,
MATT PRIME, BLAKE ANTHONY CARTER
and MAUREEN McDONALD

* Recorded a half step higher.

Call me, ba - by, if you need a friend.
Come a - long with me and don't be scared.

I just wan - na give you love. Come on, come on, come on.
I just wan - na set you free. Come on, come on, come on.

Reach - ing out to you, so take a chance. No
You and me can make it an - y - where. For

mat - ter where you go, know you're not a - lone. I'm on - ly

now, we can stay here for a while 'cause, you know,

I just wan - na see you smile. No

mat - ter where you go, you know you're not a - lone. I'm on - ly

one call a - way, I'll be there to

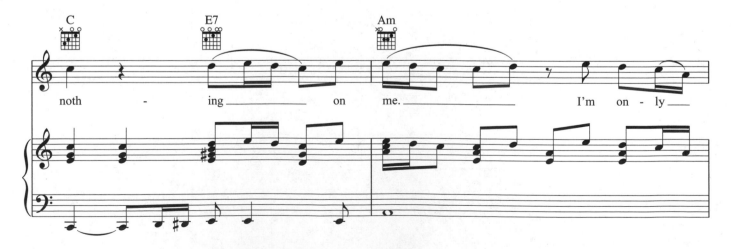

OPHELIA

Words and Music by JEREMY FRAITES
and WESLEY SCHULTZ

noth - ing back.

I, I've got a new girl - friend. She

feels like he's on top. And I _____

SAY SOMETHING

Words and Music by IAN AXEL,
CHAD VACCARINO and MIKE CAMPBELL

Say some-thing, I'm giv-ing up on you.

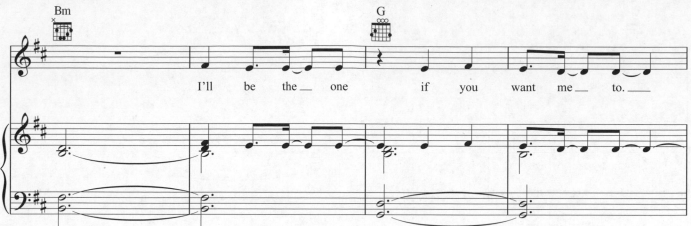

I'll be the __ one if you want me __ to. ___

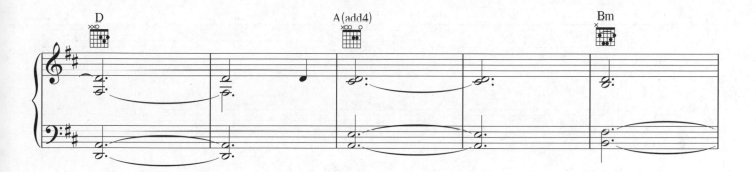

An - y - where __ I would have fol - lowed __ you. __

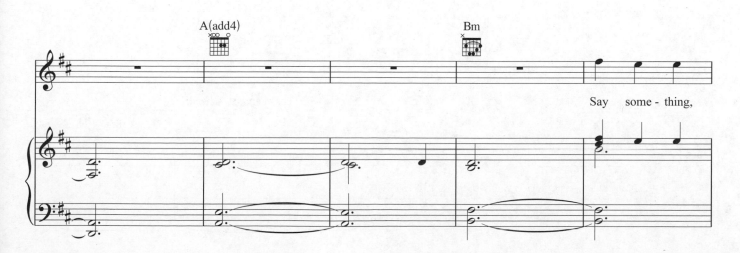

Say some - thing,

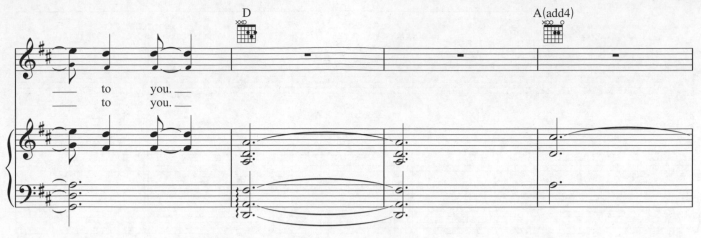

to you.
to you.

And An - y - where ___ An - y - where ___ I would have

fol - lowed ___ you. ___

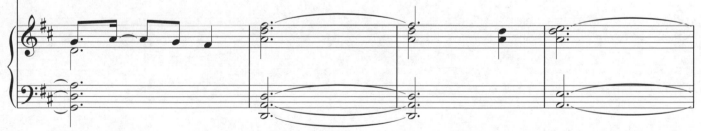

Say some - thing, I'm giv - ing up on you.

SAY YOU WON'T LET GO

Words and Music by STEVEN SOLOMON,
JAMES ARTHUR and NEIL ORMANDY

I met you in the dark, you lit me up,
I wake you up with some break-fast in bed,

you made me feel as though I was e - nough. __
I'll bring you cof - fee with a kiss on your head. __

We danced the night a - way,
And I'll take the kids to school,

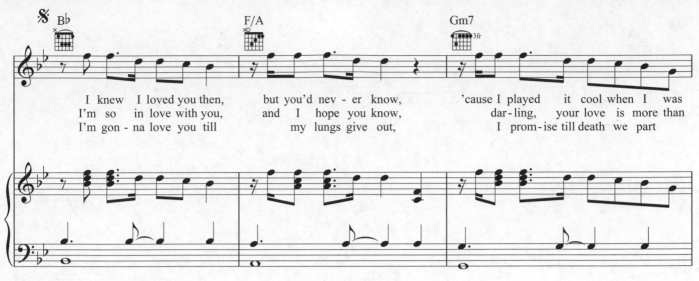

I knew I loved you then, but you'd nev - er know, 'cause I played it cool when I was
I'm so in love with you, and I hope you know, dar - ling, your love is more than
I'm gon - na love you till my lungs give out, I prom - ise till death we part

scared of let - ting go. _____ I know I need - ed you, but I nev - er showed,
worth its weight in gold. _____ We've come so far, my dear, look how we've grown,
like in our vows. _____ So I wrote this song for you, now ev - 'ry - bod - y knows

but I wan - na stay with you un - til we're gray and old. _____
and I wan - na stay with you un - til we're gray and old. _____ } Just say you_ won't let go. _____
that it's just you and me un - til we're gray and old. _____

Just say you ___ won't ___ let go. ___

I wan - na live with you   e - ven when we're ghosts, ___

'cause you were al - ways there   for me when   I   need - ed you most. ___

D.S. al Coda

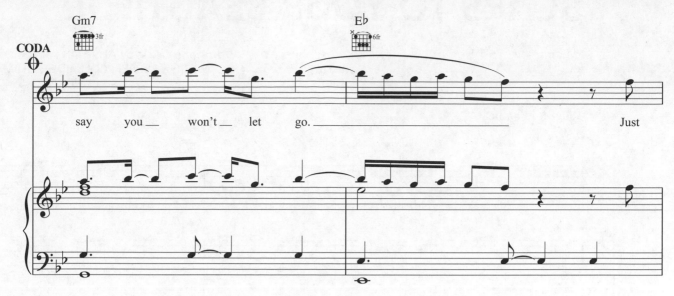

say you ___ won't ___ let go. _____ Just

say you ___ won't ___ let go. _____ Just

say you ___ won't ___ let go. _____

SCARS TO YOUR BEAUTIFUL

Words and Music by ALESSIA CARACCIOLO,
WARREN FELDER, COLERIDGE TILLMAN
and ANDREW WANSEL

deep-er than the eyes can find it. May-be we have made her blind, so

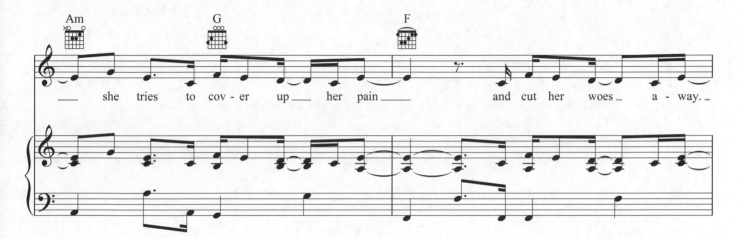

she tries to cov-er up her pain and cut her woes a-way.

'Cause cov-er girls don't cry af-ter their face is made.

But there's a hope that's wait-ing for you in the dark. You should know you're

beau - ti - ful   just the way you are.   And you don't have to change a thing; the world could change its

heart.   No scars to your beau - ti - ful.   We're stars and we're beau - ti - ful._____   Oh, __

oh. _____   Oh, _____   oh. _____

__   And you don't have to change a thing; the world could change its heart.   No scars to your beau-

ti - ful.   We're stars and we're beau - ti - ful._____   She has dreams to

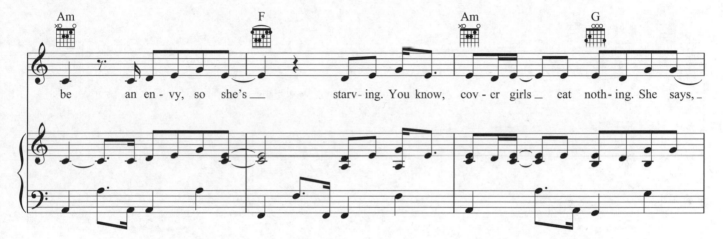

be   an en - vy, so she's __   starv - ing. You know, cov - er girls __ eat noth - ing. She says, __

__   "Beau - ty is   pain, and there's beau - ty in   ev - 'ry - thing. _ What's a lit - tle bit of hun - ger?

I can go a lit - tle while long - er."   She fades a - way. She don't   see   her "per - fect," she don't

un - der - stand_ she's worth it or that beau - ty goes deep - er than the sur - face, oh, _____

oh. _____ So, to all _____ the girls _____ that's hurt - ing, let me be your mir - ror, help you see a

lit - tle bit clear - er the light _____ that shines _____ with - in. _____ There's a

CODA

No bet - ter you than the you that you are. (No bet - ter you than the you that you are.)

No bet-ter life than the life we're liv-ing. (No bet-ter life than the life we're liv-ing.)

No bet-ter time for your shine; you're a star. (No bet-ter time for your shine; you're a star.) Oh, you're beau-

ti-ful. ___ Oh, you're beau-ti-ful. _____ There's a hope that's wait-ing for you ___ in the

dark. You should know you're beau-ti-ful just the way you are. And you don't have to

change a thing; the world could change its heart. No scars to your beau - ti - ful. We're stars and we're beau-

ti - ful. _____ Oh, ___ oh. _____ Oh, _____

oh. _____ And you don't have to change a thing; the world could change its

heart. No scars to your beau - ti - ful. We're stars and we're beau - ti - ful. _____

SEND MY LOVE
(To Your New Lover)

Words and Music by ADELE ADKINS,
MAX MARTIN and SHELLBACK

Moderate groove

for the big one,   for the big jump,   I'd be your last love, __ ev - er - last - ing,
I was run - ning,   you were walk - ing,   you could - n't keep up, __ you were fall - ing

you __ and me, __ (down,) __ mm, __ that was what you told me.
down, __ mm, __ there's on - ly one way down.

I'm __ giv - ing you __ up,   I've __ for - giv - en it __ all, __

__ you set me __ free. __

more. _____ I'm ___ giv-ing you ___ up,

I've ___ for - giv - en it ___ all, ___ you set me ___ free. ___

D.S. al Coda

N.C.

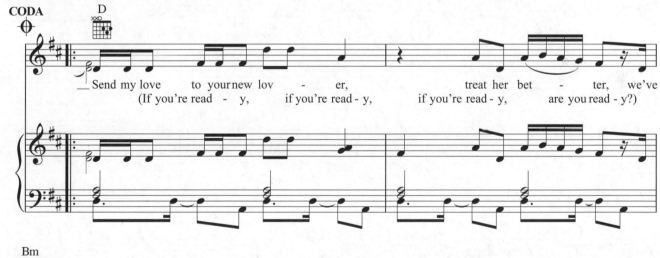

CODA

___ Send my love to your new lov - er, treat her bet - ter, we've
(If you're read - y, if you're read - y, if you're read - y, are you read - y?)

got-ta let go of all of our ghosts, _ we both know we ain't kids no more. _____

N.C.

7 YEARS

Words and Music by LUKAS FORCHHAMMER,
MORTEN RISTORP, STEFAN FORREST,
DAVID LABREL, CHRISTOPHER BROWN
and MORTEN PILEGAARD

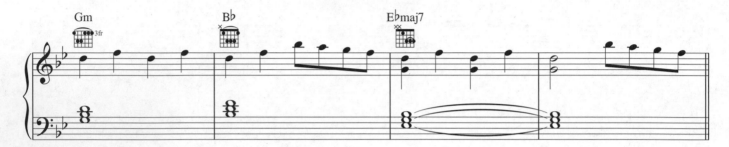

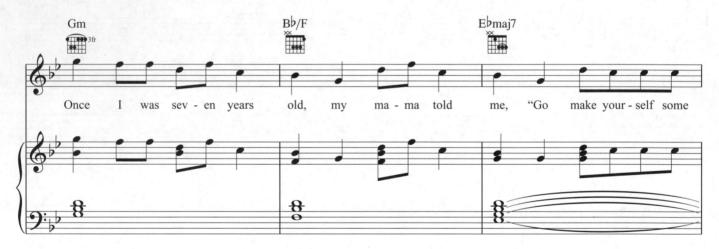

old, my dad-dy told me, "Go get your-self a wife or you'll be lone-ly." __

Once I was e-lev-en years old.

I al-ways had that __ dream __ like my dad-dy be-fore me,
I on-ly see my __ goals, __ I don't be-lieve __ in fail-ure

so I start-ed writ-ing songs, I start-ed writ-ing sto-ries.
'cause I know the small-est voic-es, they can make it ma-jor.

Some-thing a-bout that glo-ry, just al-ways seemed to bore me
I got my boys___ with me, at least___ those in fa-vor,

'cause on-ly those I real-ly love will ev-er real-ly know me.
and if we don't meet be-fore I leave, I hope I'll see you lat-er.

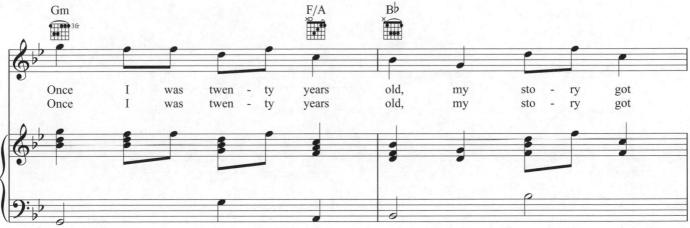

Once I was twen-ty years old, my sto-ry got
Once I was twen-ty years old, my sto-ry got

told be-fore the morn-ing sun, when life was lone-ly.___
told, I was writ-ting 'bout ev-'ry-thing I saw be-fore me.___

I'm still learn-ing a-bout life. _____ My wom-an brought chil-dren for me

so I can sing them all my songs and I can tell them sto-ries.

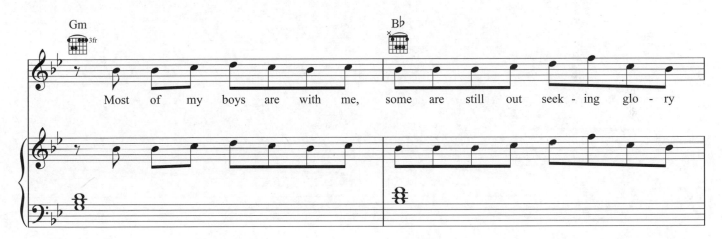

Most of my boys are with me, some are still out seek-ing glo-ry

and some I had to leave be-hind. My broth-er, I'm still sor-ry.

Soon I'll be six-ty years old. My dad-dy got six-ty - one. Re-mem-ber life and then your

life be-comes a bet-ter one. I made a man so hap-py

when I wrote a let-ter once. I hope my chil-dren come and

vis-it once or twice a month. Soon I'll be six-ty years old. Will I think the world is

cold or will I have a lot of chil-dren who can warm me?__ Soon I'll be six-ty years

old.

Soon I'll be six-ty years old.__ Will I think the world is cold or will I have a lot of

chil-dren who can hold me? Soon I'll be six-ty years old.

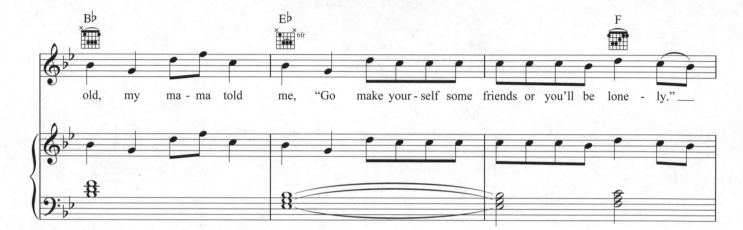

24K MAGIC

Words and Music by BRUNO MARS,
PHILIP LAWRENCE and CHRIS BROWN

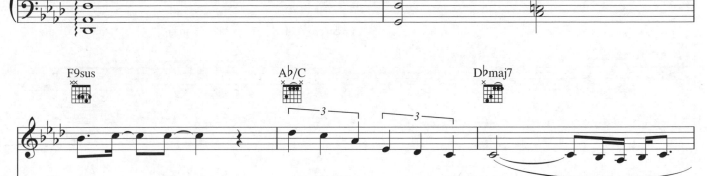

play- er. Look out!

Rap 1: (See additional lyrics)
Rap 2: (See additional lyrics)

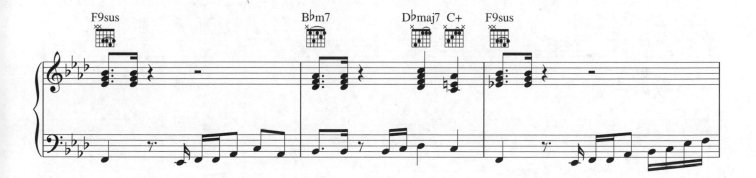

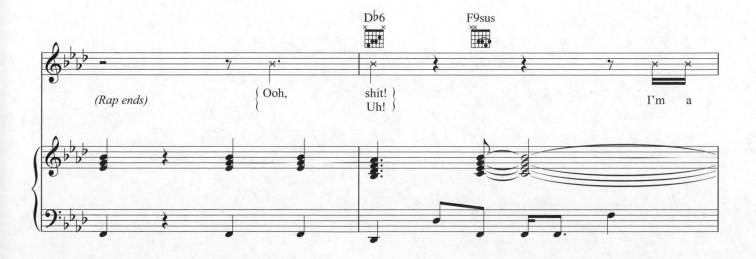

(Rap ends)

Ooh, shit!
Uh!

I'm a

Additional Lyrics

Rap 1: Pop, pop, it's show time (show time), show time (show time).
Guess who's back again.
Oh, they don't know? (Go on, tell 'em.)
They don't know? (Go on, tell 'em.)
I bet they know as soon as we walk in.
(Showin' up) wearin' Cuban links (yeah), designer minks (yeah),
Inglewood's finest shoes (whoop, whoop).
Don't look too hard; might hurt yourself.
Known to give the color red the blues.

Rap 2: Second verse for the hustlers (hustlers), gangsters (gangsters),
Bad bitches and your ugly-ass friends.
Can I preach? (Uh-oh.) Can I preach? (Uh-oh.)
I gotta show 'em how a pimp get it in.
First, take your sip (sip), do your dip (dip).
Spend your money like money ain't shit.
(Ooh, ooh, we too fresh).
Got to blame it on Jesus (#blessed).
They ain't ready for me.

SHE USED TO BE MINE

Words and Music by
SARA BAREILLES

It's not eas - y to know; __ I'm not an - y-thing like I

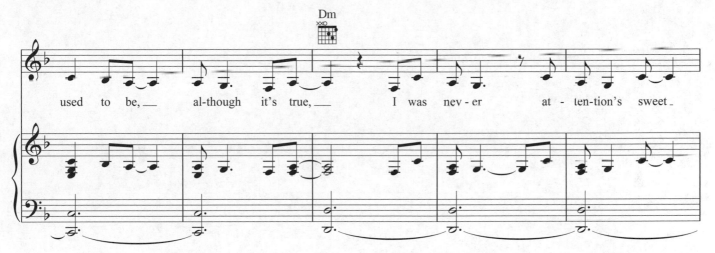

used to be, __ al-though it's true, __ I was nev - er at - ten-tion's sweet __

cen - ter. I still re - mem - ber that __ girl: __ She's im - per - fect, __

_____ but she tries. She is __ good, but she lies. __

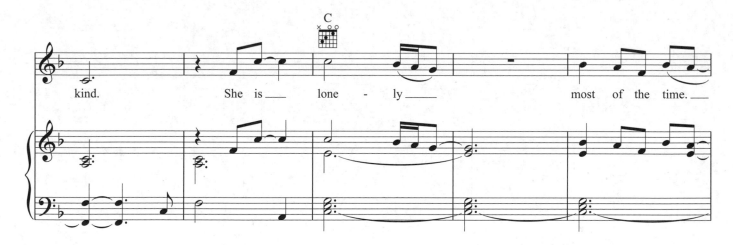

She is gone, but she used to be mine.

And it's not what I asked for.

Some-times life just slips in through a back door and

carves out a per-son and makes you be-lieve it's all true,

and now I've got you.____ And you're not____ what I asked____

____ for.____ If I'm____ hon - est, I____ know____ I would give it all

back____ for a chance____ to start o - ver and re - write____ an end-ing or____ two____

____ for the girl that I knew,____ who'd be reck - less,_____

just e-nough; who'll get __ hurt, __ but who learns how to tough-

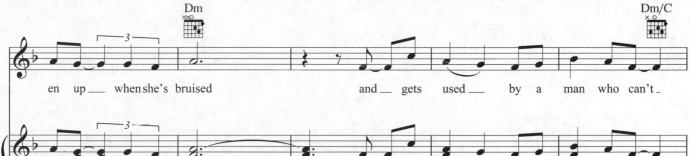

en up __ when she's bruised and __ gets used __ by a man who can't __

love. __ And then she'll get __ stuck, __ and be scared __

__ of the life that's in-side __ her, grow-ing strong-er each __ day, __ till it

fi - n'lly___ re - minds___ her to fight just___ a lit - tle to bring back the fire___

___ in her eyes ___ that's been gone, ___ but used ___ to be

mine, ___

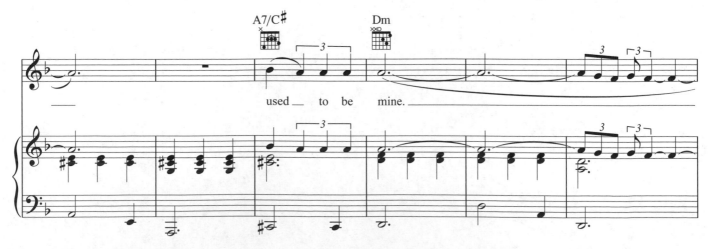

used ___ to be mine. ___

She is mess-y,

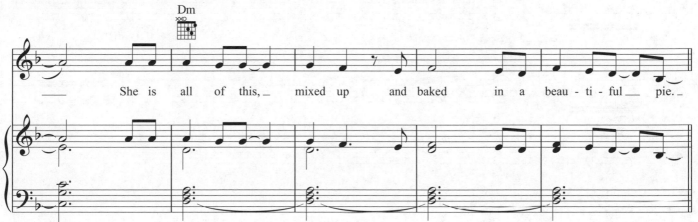

but she's kind. She is lone - ly most of the time.

She is all of this, mixed up and baked in a beau - ti - ful pie.

Freely

She is gone, but she used to be mine.

SIDE TO SIDE

Words and Music by ARIANA GRANDE,
ONIKA MARAJ, ALEXANDER KRONLUND,
MAX MARTIN, SAVAN KOTECHA and ILYA

I... I've been there all night, I've been there all

day, ___ and, boy, ___ got me walk-in' side ___ to

side. I've been there all night, I've been there all day, ___ and,

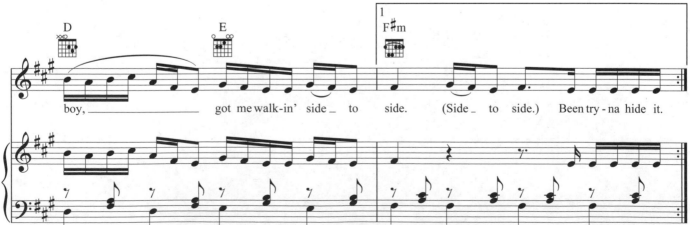

boy, ___ got me walk-in' side ___ to side. (Side ___ to side.) Been try-na hide it.

side. (Side _ to side.) This the new style _ with the fresh type of flow,

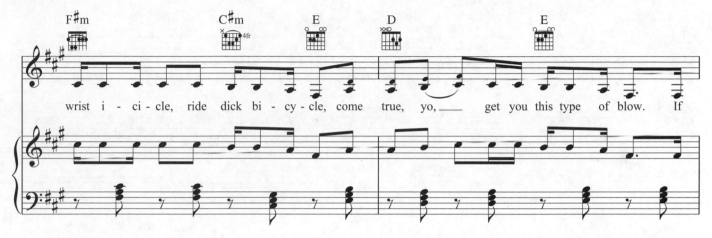

wrist i - ci - cle, ride dick bi - cy - cle, come true, yo, _ get you this type of blow. If

you wan-na Mi-naj, I got a tri - cy - cle. All these bitch-es flows with my min - i me. Bod - y smok-ing,

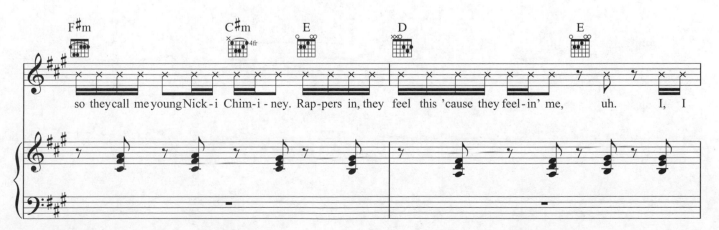

so they call me young Nick-i Chim-i-ney. Rap-pers in, they feel this 'cause they feel-in' me, uh. I, I

SIGN OF THE TIMES

Words and Music by HARRY STYLES,
JEFF BHASKER, ALEX SALIBIAN,
TYLER JOHNSON, MITCH ROWLAND
and RYAN NASCI

We got to, we got to, a - way. We

got to, we got to, a - way. We got to, we got to a - way.____

STITCHES

Words and Music by TEDDY GEIGER,
DANNY PARKER and DANIEL KYRIAKIDES

Moderate Latin groove

* *Recorded a half step lower.*

Your words cut deep - er than a knife, ___

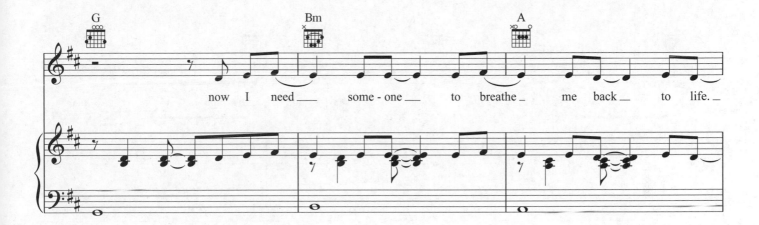

now I need ___ some - one ___ to breathe ___ me back ___ to life. ___

Got a feel - in' that I'm go - in' un - der.

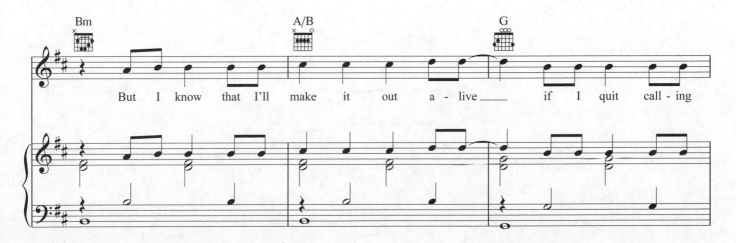

But I know that I'll make it out a - live ___ if I quit call - ing

you my lov - er and move on. _____ You watch me

bleed un - til I can't __ breathe, shak - ing. Fall - ing on - to my __ knees.

And now __ that I'm with - out __ your kiss - es, ___ I'll be need - ing stitch-

- es. ___ Trip - pin' o - ver my - self, ach - ing.

Beg - ging you to come_ help. And now_ that I'm with - out_ your kiss -

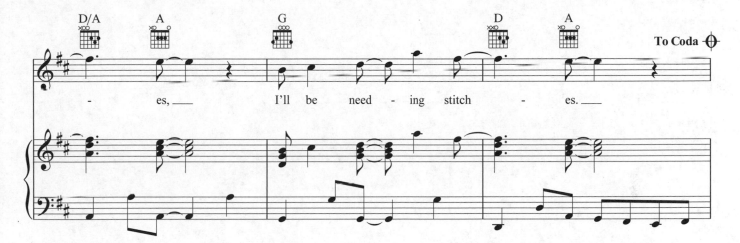

- es, ___ I'll be need - ing stitch - es. ___

To Coda

Just like a moth drawn to a flame, ___

oh, you lured _ me in, ___ I could - n't sense _ the pain. ___

Your bit-ter heart,__ cold to the touch.__

Now I'm gon-na reap___ what I___ sow. I'm left see-in' red__

__ on my__ own.___

D.S. al Coda

CODA

Nee-dle and the thread, got-ta

get you out of my head. Nee - dle and the thread, gon - na wind up dead.

Nee - dle and the thread, got - ta get you out of my head. Nee - dle and the thread, gon - na

wind up dead. Nee - dle and the thread, got - ta get you out of my head.

Nee - dle and the thread, gon - na wind up dead. Nee - dle and the thread, got - ta

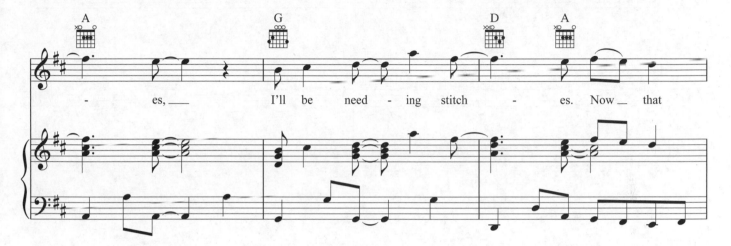

STORY OF MY LIFE

Words and Music by JAMIE SCOTT,
JOHN HENRY RYAN, JULIAN BUNETTA,
HARRY STYLES, LIAM PAYNE,
LOUIS TOMLINSON, NIALL HORAN
and ZAIN MALIK

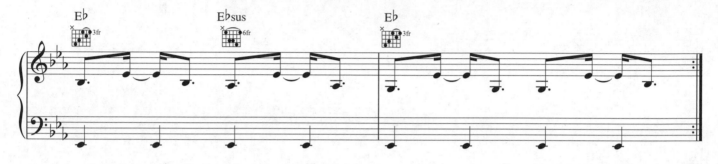

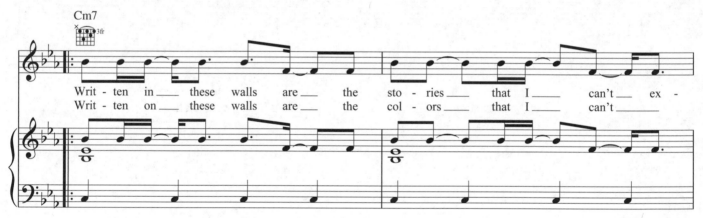

Writ-ten in these walls are the sto-ries that I can't ex-
Writ-ten on these walls are the col-ors that I can't

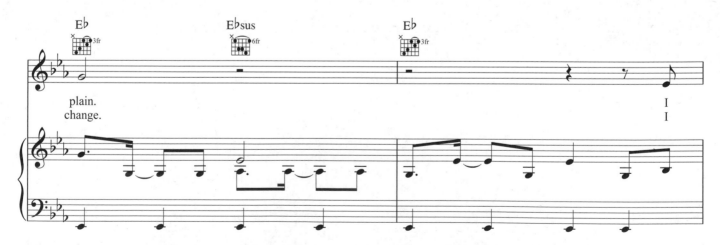

plain.
change.

I
I

leave my ___ heart o – pen, ___ but it stays right ___ here emp – ty ___ for
leave my ___ heart o – pen, ___ but it stays right ___ here ___ in ___ its

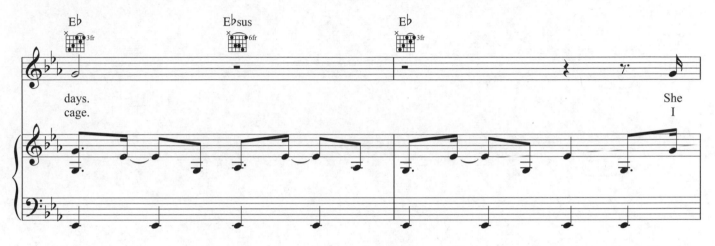

days.
cage.
She
I

told me in the morn – in' she don't feel the same a – bout ___ us in her
know that in the morn – in' now I see a sin – gle light ___ up – on the

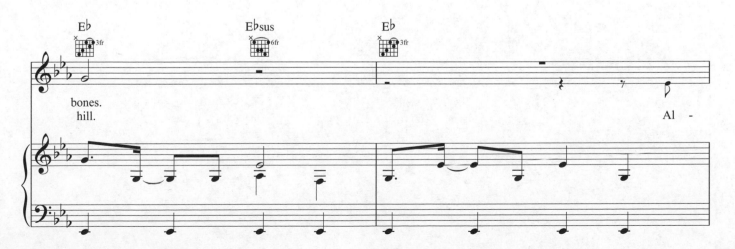

bones.
hill.
Al –

Cm7

Seems to me ___ that when I die, ___ these words will ___ be writ-ten on ___ my
though I ___ am bro - ken, my heart is ___ un - tamed _____ still. ___

A♭

E♭   E♭sus   E♭

stone. _____

And I'll ___ be
And I'll ___ be

A♭   B♭   Cm

gone,   gone to - night. _____   The ground be - neath ___ my
gone,   gone to - night. _____   The fire be - neath ___ my

A♭   B♭   Cm

feet is o - pen wide, _____   the way that I've ___ been
feet is burn - in' bright, ___   the way that I've ___ been

hold - in' on _____ too tight _____ with noth - in' in ____ be -
hold - in' on _____ so tight _____ with noth - in' in ____ be -

tween.
tween.

The

sto - ry of ____ my life. I take her ____ home. ____ I

drive all ____ night ____ to keep her ____ warm _____ and time ____

is like chas - in' the clouds. _____ The

sto - ry of ___ my life. I take her ___ home. ___ I

drive all ___ night ___ to keep her ___ warm. ___ And time ___ is

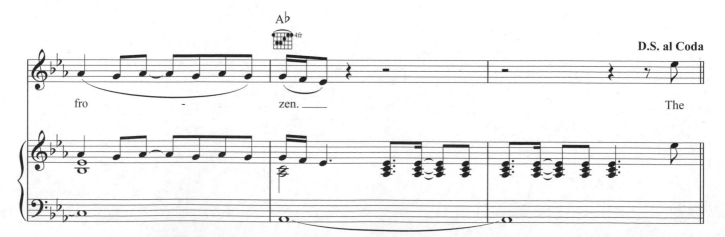

fro - zen. ___ The

D.S. al Coda

WAKE ME UP

Words and Music by ALOE BLACC,
TIM BERGLING and MICHAEL EINZIGER

up when it's __ all o - ver, when I'm wis - er and __ I'm old -

- er. All this time I was find - in' __ my - self and I __

did - n't know __ I __ was lost. So wake me up when it's __ all o -

- ver, when I'm wis - er and I'm old - er. __ All this

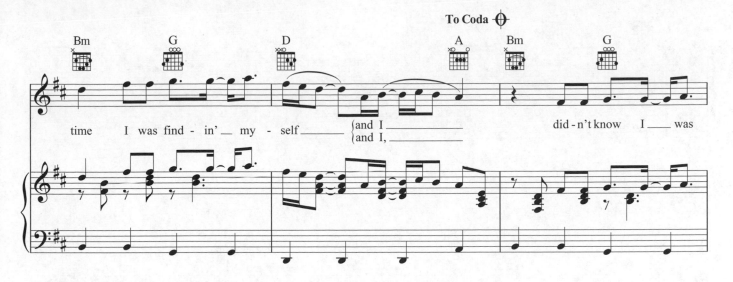

time I was find - in' __ my - self _____ {and I _____ {and I, _____ did - n't know I ___ was

lost. _____

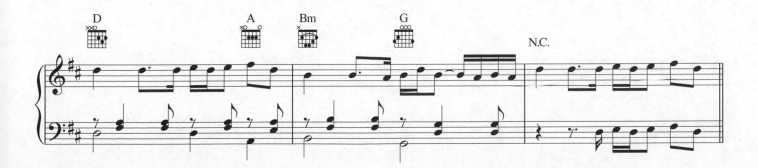

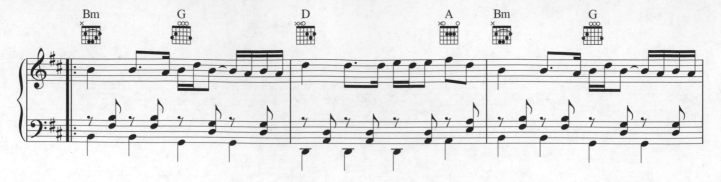

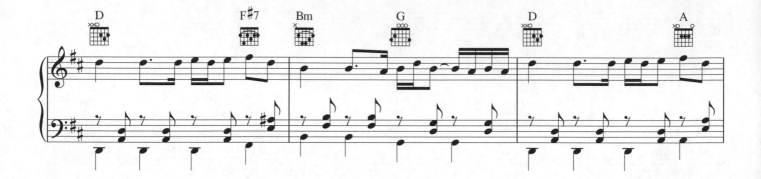

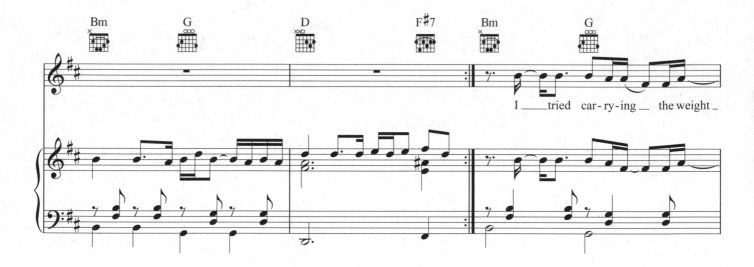

I ___ tried car-ry-ing ___ the weight ___

___ of ___ the world, ___ but I on-ly have ___ two hands. ___

CODA

I did-n't know_ I___ was lost.___

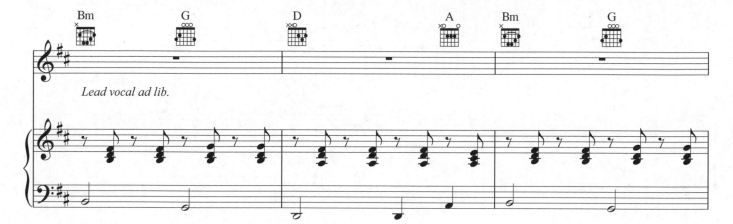

Lead vocal ad lib.

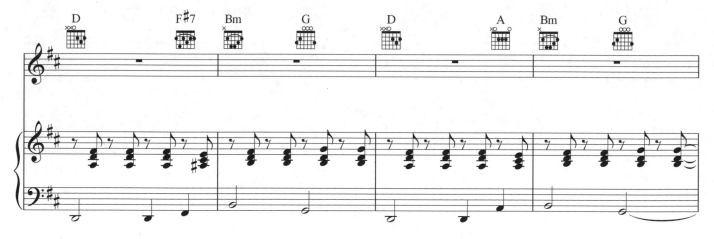

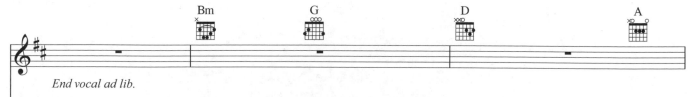

End vocal ad lib.

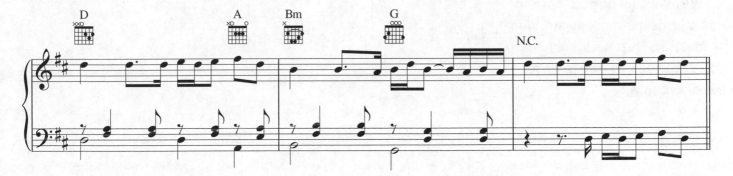

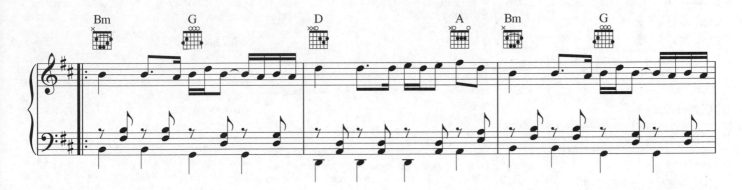

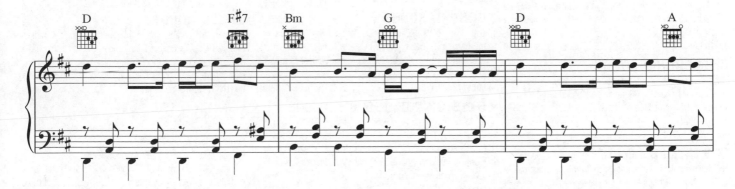

Get more BANG for your buck!

budgetbooks

These value-priced collections feature **over 300 pages** of **piano/vocal/guitar** arrangements. With at least **70 hit songs** in most books, you pay **18 cents or less** for each song!

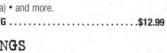

ACOUSTIC
66 unplugged jewels: American Pie • Black-bird • Leaving on a Jet Plane • More Than Words • Scarborough Fair • Tears in Heaven • Time in a Bottle • Wonderwall • more.
00311857 P/V/G $14.99

ACOUSTIC HITS
Make the most out of your money with this collection of 58 hits: Bridge over Troubled Water • Falling Slowly • Hallelujah • Love Story • The Night They Drove Old Dixie Down • Wish You Were Here • and more.
00103681 P/V/G $12.99

BLUES SONGS
99 blues classics packed into one affordable collection! Includes: All Your Love • Born Under a Bad Sign • Killing Floor • Pride and Joy • Sweet Home Chicago • The Thrill Is Gone • more!
00311499 P/V/G $14.99

BROADWAY SONGS
This jam-packed collection features 73 songs from 56 shows, including: Any Dream Will Do • Cabaret • Getting to Know You • I Dreamed a Dream • One • People • You'll Never Walk Alone • and more.
00310832 P/V/G $14.99

CHILDREN'S SONGS
This fabulous collection includes over 100 songs that kids love, including: Alphabet Song • London Bridge • On Top of Spaghetti • Sesame Street Theme • You've Got a Friend in Me • and more.
00311054 P/V/G $14.99

CHRISTMAS SONGS
100 holiday favorites, includes: All I Want for Christmas Is You • Away in a Manger • Feliz Navidad • The First Noel • Merry Christmas, Darling • O Holy Night • Silver Bells • What Child Is This? • and more.
00310887 P/V/G $14.99

CLASSIC ROCK
A priceless collection of 70 of rock's best at a price that can't be beat! Includes: Ballroom Blitz • Bohemian Rhapsody • Gloria • Pink Houses • Rhiannon • Roxanne • Summer of '69 • Wild Thing • You Really Got Me • and more.
00310906 P/V/G $14.99

CONTEMPORARY CHRISTIAN
52 CCM faves in a value-priced songbook: All to You • Be Near • Breathe • Deeper • I Wanna Sing • King • Maker of All Things • Oceans from the Rain • Pray • Song of Love • These Hands • Wisdom • more.
00311732 P/V/G $12.95

COUNTRY SONGS
A great collection of 90 songs, including: Always on My Mind • Amazed • Boot Scootin' Boogie • Down at the Twist and Shout • Friends in Low Places • Okie from Muskogee • Sixteen Tons • Walkin' After Midnight • You Are My Sunshine • and more.
00310833 P/V/G $14.99

FOLK SONGS
148 of your all-time folk favorites! Includes: Camptown Races • Danny Boy • Greensleeves • Home on the Range • Shenandoah • Skip to My Lou • Yankee Doodle • and many more.
00311841 P/V/G $12.99

GOSPEL SONGS
Over 100 songs, including: Behold the Lamb • Down by the Riverside • Daddy Sang Bass • In Times like These • Midnight Cry • We Are So Blessed • The Wonder of It All • and many more.
00311734 P/V/G $12.99

HITS OF THE 1990S & 2000S
52 hits, including: All I Wanna Do • Bleeding Love • Crazy • Hey There Delilah • Ironic • Losing My Religion • Photograph • Since U Been Gone • Smooth • Take Me Out • Unwell • Who Will Save Your Soul • With Arms Wide Open • Wonderwall • and more.
00110582 P/V/G $12.99

HYMNS
150 beloved hymns in a money-saving collection: Amazing Grace • Come, Thou Fount of Every Blessing • For the Beauty of the Earth • Holy, Holy, Holy • O Worship the King • What a Friend We Have in Jesus • many more!
00311587 P/V/G $12.99

JAZZ STANDARDS
A collection of over 80 jazz classics. Includes: Alfie • Bewitched • Blue Skies • Body and Soul • Fever • I'll Be Seeing You • In the Mood • Isn't It Romantic? • Mona Lisa • Stella by Starlight • When Sunny Gets Blue • and more.
00310830 P/V/G $14.99

LATIN SONGS
An invaluable collection of over 80 Latin standards. Includes: Desafinado (Off Key) • Frenesí • How Insensitive (Insensatez) • La Bamba • Perfidia • Spanish Eyes • So Nice (Summer Samba) • and more.
00311056 P/V/G $12.99

LOVE SONGS
This collection of over 70 favorite love songs includes: And I Love Her • Crazy • Endless Love • Longer • (You Make Me Feel Like) A Natural Woman • You Are So Beautiful • You Are the Sunshine of My Life • and more.
00310834 P/V/G $12.99

MOVIE SONGS
Over 70 memorable movie moments, including: Almost Paradise • Cole's Song • Funny Girl • Puttin' On the Ritz • She • Southampton • Take My Breath Away (Love Theme) • Up Where We Belong • The Way We Were • and more.
00310831 P/V/G $12.99

POP/ROCK
This great collection of 75 top pop hits features: Barbara Ann • Crimson and Clover • Dust in the Wind • Hero • Jack and Diane • Lady Marmalade • Stand by Me • Tequila • We Got the Beat • What's Going On • and more.
00310835 P/V/G $12.99

STANDARDS
Nearly 80 standards, including: Boogie Woogie Bugle Boy • Don't Get Around Much Anymore • In the Still of the Night • Misty • Pennies from Heaven • So in Love • What a Diff'rence a Day Made • Witchcraft • and more.
00311853 P/V/G $14.99

HAL•LEONARD®
www.halleonard.com

0619
083

THE BEST EVER
COLLECTION
ARRANGED FOR PIANO, VOICE AND GUITAR

100 of the Most Beautiful Piano Solos Ever
100 songs
00102787 .... $27.50

150 of the Most Beautiful Songs Ever
150 ballads
00360735 .... $27.00

More of the Best Acoustic Rock Songs Ever
69 tunes
00311738 .... $19.95

Best Acoustic Rock Songs Ever
65 acoustic hits
00310984 .... $22.99

Best Big Band Songs Ever
66 favorites
00286933 .... $19.99

Best Blues Songs Ever
73 blues tunes
00312874 .... $19.99

Best Broadway Songs Ever
83 songs
00309155 .... $24.99

More of the Best Broadway Songs Ever
82 songs
00311501 .... $22.95

Best Children's Songs Ever
101 songs
00159272 .... $19.99

Best Christmas Songs Ever
69 holiday favorites
00359130 .... $27.50

Best Classic Rock Songs Ever
64 hits
00289313 .... $24.99

Best Classical Music Ever
86 classical favorites
00310674 (Piano Solo) $19.95

The Best Country Rock Songs Ever
52 hits
00118881 .... $19.99

Best Country Songs Ever
78 classic country hits
00359135 .... $19.99

Best Disco Songs Ever
50 songs
00312565 .... $19.99

Best Early Rock 'n' Roll Songs Ever
74 songs
00310816 .... $19.95

Best Easy Listening Songs Ever
75 mellow favorites
00359193 .... $22.99

Best Folk/Pop Songs Ever
66 hits
00138299 .... $19.99

Best Gospel Songs Ever
80 gospel songs
00310503 .... $19.99

Best Hymns Ever
118 hymns
00310774 .... $18.99

Best Jazz Piano Solos Ever
80 songs
00312079 .... $19.99

Best Jazz Standards Ever
77 jazz hits
00311641 .... $19.95

Best Latin Songs Ever
67 songs
00310355 .... $19.99

Best Love Songs Ever
62 favorite love songs
00359198 .... $19.99

Best Movie Songs Ever
71 songs
00310063 .... $19.99

Best Movie Soundtrack Songs Ever
70 songs
00146161 .... $19.99

Best Pop/Rock Songs Ever
50 classics
00138279 .... $19.99

Best Praise & Worship Songs Ever
80 all-time favorites
00311057 .... $22.99

Best R&B Songs Ever
66 songs
00310184 .... $19.95

Best Rock Songs Ever
63 songs
00490424 .... $18.95

Best Songs Ever
71 must-own classics
00265721 .... $24.99

Best Soul Songs Ever
70 hits
00311427 .... $19.95

Best Standards Ever, Vol. 1 (A-L)
72 beautiful ballads
00359231 .... $17.95

Best Standards Ever, Vol. 2 (M-Z)
73 songs
00359232 .... $17.99

Best Wedding Songs Ever
70 songs
00290985 .... $19.99

HAL•LEONARD®
Visit us online
for complete songlists at
www.halleonard.com